3830   11-11-96

A Memory for Wonders

Mother Veronica Namoyo Le Goulard, P.C.C.

A Memory for Wonders

A True Story

Foreword by Mother Mary Francis, P.C.C.

IGNATIUS PRESS   SAN FRANCISCO

Cover design by Roxanne Mei Lum
Cover photograph by John Hawkins / Tony Stone Worldwide

© 1993 Ignatius Press, San Francisco
ISBN 0–89870–430–8
Library of Congress catalogue number 92–74110
Printed in the United States of America

Contents

Foreword

Why does one write an autobiography? There would need to be a driving force. And there are variants on that. To present oneself in neon lights, because one is a celebrity of sorts, could perhaps net one spending money *usque in saeculum*, although the "*saeculum*" itself might well be rendered dubious. Then, there could be the noncelebrity outstandingly unequipped as a writer who is irresistibly drawn to discourse by pen on that fascinating subject of self to the extent of several volumes, from which the world is saved by reason of a notable want of enthusiasm in the publishing world. And then there is also the one who writes an autobiography in painful humility, so that the world may know the wonders of God. This is such a work. We can be grateful that such wonders of God as are here revealed are confided to us by one who is already a writer of distinction.

All human lives are mysteries of God's love. And, in the deepest sense, while hidden in the folds of each one's being, they yet belong to the whole Mystical Body of Christ of which we are all members. Some lives are perhaps somewhat more astonishingly mysterious than others, at least in the sense of being more surprising. The life of Mother Veronica Namoyo Le Goulard is one of these. Having entered the Poor Clare monastery in Algiers at the age of twenty-two, after a life than can hardly be described as less than amazing by anyone, Lucette Le Goulard later became the abbess there and went on to found a monastery of Poor Clares in

Lilongwe, Malawi, a monastery now abounding in members and world-famous for its intelligently grace-directed and therefore successful inculturation.

After a silvery span of years as abbess in Malawi, Mother Veronica Namoyo returned to France in happy anticipation of ending her earthly days in a deeply hidden life of contemplation. She had hoped that God's grace would achieve a fully native community in Malawi by that time, and her hope had not been confounded. Her hope for disappearing from the eyes of men, however, was less notably fulfilled. For she was soon recalled by Rome to Africa, this time to refound a dying community in Lusaka. Abbess there for many years, during which the reestablishment of a healthy Poor Clare enclosed contemplative life was well realized, she then insisted that the abbatial leadership be entrusted to a native African. It was in this Lusaka monastery that Mother Veronica Namoyo then continued her invaluable services to God and the Church and the Order of Poor Clares as vicaress and novice mistress and first councilor of an African Federation of Poor Clares, having earlier been the first federal abbess of the initial federation there.

Lucette was given the name "Veronica" at her Poor Clare investiture. To this was well added by an African archbishop the descriptive name "Namoyo", that is, "the life-bringer". It is an apt description of the woman who bears it. The first native African abbesses in Lilongwe and Lusaka are the two whom Mother Veronica Namoyo received as her first postulants.

This autobiography was written at the more than earnest request of the African abbess in Lusaka as being the only gift she desired for the celebration of her silver jubilee several years ago. It was intended to be a private gift reserved to the community in Lusaka. I entered the scene when Mother

Veronica Namoyo, one of my dearest friends, entrusted the manuscript to me for some editing. A native Frenchwoman who has had limited opportunities to exercise her writing and speaking of English these many years past in Africa, she felt the writing needed perhaps some grammatical surveillance. When I realized what a treasure was in my hands, what a dazzling exposition of God's amazing work, I joined forces with Mother Josefa, the young African abbess in Lusaka, to persuade Mother Veronica Namoyo to allow me to submit it for publication. Mother Veronica Namoyo fought a very good initial fight against this proposal.

Part of my own service as federal abbess of the United States of America Federation of Mary Immaculate was to invite some British Poor Clare abbesses, two of them officers of the Association of Poor Clares in England, as guests to our federation chapter held in Roswell in 1987. Permission was readily obtained from higher authority to make this enriching exchange and interchange possible. The invitation was also extended to the English-speaking abbess president of the Poor Clare Federation in Africa (who was unable to accept it) and to the first federal councilor there, who, happily for us, was able to accept it. This was Mother Veronica Namoyo.

One afternoon during the chapter days in Roswell, I sat alone with Mother Veronica in our modest office room to engage in a serious debate. Long one in spirit, heart and ideal, and usually in opinions also, we now found ourselves at direct odds. I felt that this autobiography entrusted to me in a special way could not be withheld from a wide reading public. Mother Veronica would have none of this. It was private. It was not for distribution. It was assuredly not for publication. We sat for a while in a confrontational silence, words dropping away before a direct, if silent, slamming of two disparate ideas, the one against the other. Then, finally, I spoke again.

Mother Veronica Namoyo has long been very kind in her assessments of my own poetry, rejoicing my heart with her understanding of whatever it is I have tried to express. I thanked her again for this and recalled to her that, if one is going to write anything even resembling true poetry, one must agree to be very poor. Poetry reveals the inmost soul and heart of the singer, if it is poetry at all. If one writes poetry, one must give oneself away. I reminded Mother Veronica Namoyo, too, of the great attraction God had long since given her to profound poverty. Having long and faithfully responded to this attraction of grace in ways made clear in this autobiography, I asked by what right before God she could keep this manuscript for herself and a few. I inquired how she would justify keeping secret such wondrous works of God as could draw many souls to fall down in adoration before the wonder of his ways. I saw what she had written as an evident channel of grace for many and asked her to relinquish any ownership of the works of God in her life. I suggested that this might be the epitome of poverty to which God had invited her—to abdicate that last holding.

Mother Veronica bent her head. After a few moments she said, "I trust you absolutely. I will do it." I hold that moment as among the most cherished of my life.

So, here is the relinquishing of her privacy in a truly marvelous tale of God's grace. We would doubtless prefer that it not end at the enclosure doors of a Poor Clare monastery in Africa. We would like to know all about the ongoing wonders of grace in her life as a cloistered contemplative Poor Clare nun. Yet on this I would never debate nor even attempt to persuade. Perhaps when her earthly course is run, some others will write of her Poor Clare life. After her insistence on leaving the service of abbess in favor of a native African Poor Clare for some years, the native Africans insisted on reclaiming their first spiritual mother. Once again abbess in Lusaka, Mother Veronica Namoyo goes on doing what she has always done since first struck down by grace when she was three years old: worshipping God and inviting with irresistible sincerity and love others to do the same.

Mother Mary Francis, P.C.C.

"He makes us remember his wonders. . . ."
Psalm 111

Chapter I

Roots

My roots are all in Brittany, the very tip of Brittany where land and sea meet at the end of Europe. For centuries my ancestors were Bretons, Celtic sons and daughters of a land almost surrounded by the ocean, daring people on giant killing waves, fighting people in storms and shipwrecks, poor people on fields robbed of topsoil by raging winds and constant rains, silent people used to hardship, distrustful of strangers and spare with their rock-sounding words. But when they did speak, it was not without kindness and sometimes shy tenderness, perhaps all the deeper for being so discreetly expressed, like the beauty of this land where the colors blend so delicately that it needs your full attention to discern whether the mauve of the sky is not turning to blue or pink, whether the water in the creek is turquoise or green.

When I was born, many women were still wearing, at least on feast days, their gaily embroidered regional costumes and, on their long auburn or golden hair, lace caps, different for each village. On Sundays, farmers put on their short velvet jackets and ribboned hats. But most of the men were fishermen. They were on the sea for months, while their mothers and wives waited anxiously for them to return, too often in vain, as many perished and were buried in the

immensity of water. I did not hear much laughing or talking, but there was joy at the rare festive gatherings with vio-
lins, bagpipes and dances or, in summer, during the walks on
the small hills covered with purple briars or sunlit with
brooms.

I had little time to know all this because I did not dwell
long in Brittany and because this region was changing fast,
but I always sensed that I was a daughter of a rugged,
cragged land and of the mysterious ocean. When God called
me to a cloister in Algeria, I found it very difficult to
renounce forever even the hope of seeing the ocean again.

On the side of my mother, Anne Le Théo, my ancestors
were all sailors. My grandfather was tall, slim and strong. For
me he was almost a mythical hero, who had gone everywhere in the world, escaped death under hundreds of guises
and knew every skill and science! He could repair clocks
and motors, tailor a suit, make shoes or chairs. He smoked a
big pipe (which choked me when he jokingly invited me to
try it). Jumping into a small boat, he was able to steer it to its
destination among reefs just by shifting his weight from
right to left. He held me entranced with scores of feats like
this and many more tricks or with stories of his journeys. At
ten he was with the famous Iceland fishermen. He almost
froze to death while keeping vigils on the foremast in a
small basket hung very high, where only a child could
remain among ropes and sails, looking at grey skies and
mighty waves or threatening icebergs. Later on he was even
part of the crew of a boat that carried French criminals to
Guyana in America. There were tempests and mutinies to
make the journeys less monotonous. Then he was in the
State Marine for a while, and on parade days he still wore a
resplendent uniform that seemed to me like the attire of a
king, complete with a ceremonial sword. Finally he had his

own boat with a crew of eight men. They went far and deep and gloried in more shipwrecks than Saint Paul. It was fascinating to have such a grandfather, half-legendary while still living. He was retired, however, when I knew him in the great city of Brest, where I was born: a town that lived off the ocean, too, and a military port of great strategic importance. It was on this account that the city was totally destroyed during the war of 1939–1945 and had to be rebuilt.

In my grandfather's time, warships, steamers and many other boats were constantly moving into the great bay or out of its calm waters. And grandfather, together with some other weather-beaten "sea wolves", as they were called, watched these boats for hours, criticizing the new generations of sailors, who had such an easy life with their motors but were just "soft-water sailors" (a great insult in Brittany).

I don't remember my maternal grandmother. From her photos she was a small, graceful woman in traditional costume. Like most Bretons of the time, she was very attached to her religious traditions and faith. So was her own father, who was still living. Grandfather himself had left his religious practice in some far-away sea, though he still believed in God; but for grandmother, faith was essential, and she lived according to strict Christian principles. As we were to be alienated later on from this part of the family, I do not remember if my mother had two or three brothers, but she was the only daughter. All these children were bright and successful in their studies. One of them was to become the youngest warrant officer in the French naval army; but one day, when a visiting higher officer humiliated him in public, he reacted by slapping that officer on the face. He was immediately degraded, and he entered the Foreign Legion, a famous corps of reckless soldiers.

Her other brother had a normal career, and my mother grew into a very beautiful and gifted girl. She was preparing for the equivalent of the Grade 12 examinations here, with one more year of studies ahead of her, when something happened that is difficult to understand outside of the context of French history.

The persecution of the Catholic Church by the French government (Combes) at the beginning of the twentieth century resulted in the expulsion of many religious congregations. The Church lost much of her holdings (a blessing in disguise), and in some regions a bitter struggle started between the Catholic and government schools. The "school dispute" is still going on in France. Just after the First World War, a new generation of teachers was beginning to work there in government schools. Almost all of them had lost their Christian faith, thanks to the formation received at their teacher-training colleges. In Brittany the conflict divided groups and families, as the government was showing an almost fanatical anticlericalism and the Church was hardening her position.

My future mother was a happy student in the much-respected government school in her part of the town. The teachers were good and quite neutral. Like most of her schoolmates, she went regularly to Mass but was not particularly interested in religious studies or activities. She wanted success, more freedom and money enough to do what pleased her. She worked well and enjoyed being pretty, without falling into reprehensible behavior. There was also a Catholic school in the neighborhood, but the teachers were underqualified and underpaid, and most of the students were failing their exams. It had never been a question of my mother going there. In any case, nothing against her faith had ever been attempted where she was.

Then, like a bolt of lightning, came an "ordinance" from the Bishop of Quimper enjoining all Christian parents to put their children into Catholic-sponsored schools under pain of excommunication! Parents with children in government schools (the only places where they did not have to pay fees) could not receive any of the sacraments. My grandfather was greatly angered by this dictatorial procedure and said that he would never take Anne from her school. Anne herself felt relieved. She wanted to succeed in her examinations; and she, too, thought that the Bishop was using unfair and harsh means to impose his decisions. My grandmother suffered much. She asked her husband to change his mind, but he refused, so both of them were automatically excommunicated. By then they had another serious concern: grandmother had hidden a developing breast cancer for two years. Because of Christian "modesty" or decency, as it was then understood, she could not bring herself to show her chest to a doctor. But my grandfather discovered the terrible wound and immediately called a physician. The latter said that he had been called too late but still counseled an operation. He made it clear, however, that grandmother could die on the operating table. She was still under fifty but much weakened by this illness. Then began her calvary. If it had depended on her, she would have transferred her daughter to the Catholic school, but my grandfather was adamantly opposed to this move. She went to all the priests in the numerous parishes of this large Catholic city and explained her case. No one gave her absolution. I doubt she needed it, as she had always been loving, dutiful and generously self-giving; but, for her, to be excommunicated meant to be condemned to hell. Thus she went to the hospital. Fortunately the operation was a half-success. It prolonged her life for two or three years, enough to enable Anne to

complete her schooling, so that grandmother finally died
with the sacraments that had been so cruelly denied her. I
am glad to say that Rome did not condone the Bishop's
attitude. The regulations he had imposed were withdrawn.
But it was too late for the faith of many. Grandfather and
his daughter were so revolted that they promised never to
enter a church again, and they lost all interest in God and in
his priests, except when they had the opportunity of joining
the Church's enemies.

Let us leave Anne to pass her examinations with honors
and start a career in the Post Office, while dreams of marriage came with her sixteenth year and her maturing beauty
and charm.

On my father's side, we have quite different people. Both
Grandfather and Grandmother Le Goulard were teachers
and so were their four children: my Aunts Marcelle and
Jeanne, my Uncle Albert and my future father, Lucien. The
family owned a one-story house made of solid grey granite
with a back garden and orchard. This was to remain the
"family house", large and, in our sight, beautiful, though
modest by modern standards. Its dwellers were rather good
people, interested in politics, discoveries and sometimes in
books, though none more so than my father, who was unan-
imously considered the most intelligent of a clan for whom
intelligence was a virtue. Honesty of course was taken for
granted. He came out of the First World War an ardent
socialist, pacifist and a convinced atheist, and soon after he
had everybody on his side, thinking that the Church was the
institution responsible for most of the social evils of the
time, that religious "superstitions" had to be uprooted everywhere and universal socialism established on the foundations
laid by well-led workers' unions linked with an intellectual
elite. He was himself a born leader.

Grandfather approved but spent his own time as a retired civil servant more in his garden and his workshop than in political meetings. He had many fruit trees to tend, gorgeous dahlias and chrysanthemums, and he could make charming doll's furniture for his grandchildren. Grandmother stopped going to Mass for fear that her sons would number her among the "reactionaries" they should fight, but it was not without remorse. Uncle Albert followed my father enthusiastically, Aunt Marcelle had little faith anyway, and Aunt Jeanne was unable to resist her cherished "little brother" and was always seduced by generous ideas of justice, freedom and enlightenment. They were wont to speak of the "proletariat", but they were not proletarians, with their big house, the large cupboards filled with embroidered linen (at seventy, grandmother had still not slept in all her dowry sheets) and the beautiful dining room, where twelve persons were at ease at the oak table, facing a large carved sideboard and surrounded with high-backed chairs. We had a smaller dining room for daily use, and life was simple enough. It was several years after my birth that running water and electricity were added to the comforts of the rooms. Before this, the servant, "Little Marie", was on the go fetching water from the public pump down the street. Marie was a small peasant woman, always apparelled in long black dresses and white lace cap, very ignorant of worldly science but discreet, prayerful and always ready for the task at hand. Sometimes this was almost beyond her strength, like washing all the linen each month at the wash house and carrying it back still wet, bending for half a kilometer under the heavy burden. She slept in a very small room and had holy pictures above her bed. Grandmother did not want her to be persecuted for that, so her room was always locked. If she had been forbidden to go to Mass, she would probably have left the family, though she was very devoted to all of us.

Though in the same town, my two sets of grandparents lived in different worlds, but eventually Lucien met Anne and they fell in love with each other. Though Anne looked fifteen and was barely two years more, they decided to marry in August 1921. Both of them were eager to taste the independence that was then denied to unmarried youth. They also wanted to enjoy their life together for quite a long time without having children; but disturbing their serene plan for the future, I announced my coming some months after their marriage, to the consternation of my young parents and the delight of both their own families.

I was born on May 11, 1922. I was told during my childhood that there was a storm that day with high waves and winds that might have had an unfavorable influence on my character! The fact is, I was born without much fuss and named Luce (or Lucette) after my father. In years to come I was to choose Saint Luke as my patron saint and to love him very much.

I was not strong and my mother could not nurse me, so I was entrusted for a time to my grandparents, and they had me baptized in church, while father was preparing a new place for the family to live in a small town, Chateaulin, not far away. It was quite a plot. Grandmother Le Théo, who was slowly dying from her cancer, could not resign herself to leaving a pagan granddaughter behind her. She obtained the complicity of her husband, because he was sorry to have hurt her over the school disagreement, and he was pleased to be godfather. Then Grandmother Le Goulard was also bribed into being godmother, and Little Marie was a very busy intermediary with the parish. The other members of the clan withdrew in silence, waiting for the return of the blissfully unknowing parents. So it was that, born from declared atheists and fiercely anticlerical parents, I was baptized at Saint Louis church on June 4, 1922. We would probably not approve of this procedure; but it was inspired, I believe, in its uncanonical way. I have always considered the other graces I received through the years, in spite of their sometimes exceptional character, as the mere development of this one, the greatest.

My parents, of course, were furious, so much so that they decided to leave Brittany as soon as possible, so that "nobody could speak to me of God, and no one could influence the development of my mind with oppressive superstition." Moreover, they made Grandmother Le Goulard promise solemnly that she would never say a word to me in future years about religious faith of any kind, else she would be forever separated from her beloved son. As for Grandmother Le Théo, she was serenely dying a holy death, and she surely asked the Lord to make me know him one day.

My father was also feeling that he needed more scope for his energies, and he decided to go to Morocco, which had been entrusted to France as a "protectorate" after the war. It was an adventurous choice, as the east of the country had not been "pacified". It is difficult to see why these powerful Arab *Kaids* in their armed castles or lavishly decorated palaces were in need of French "protection".

I was two years old when I left Brittany, and I dimly remember one thing: my great-grandfather kissing me in tears. As a child I was to tell my friends: "You have only four grandparents, but I had five, and one of them cried when I left him." Somehow this old man made me conscious of being loved. My parents loved me, too, but were so involved in their own desires and activities, so young and unprepared, that they never gave me this warm feeling. As a result, I was to grow into a "difficult child".

Chapter II

Childhood in Morocco

I do not remember anything more about family or journeys during this period, but my parents told me afterward what happened within my first months in Africa. They had to settle for two or three years, as was normal for French "beginners" there, in one of the worst parts of beautiful Morocco: the eastern part, near the frontier on the railway line to Algiers. There were few Europeans there. Tante Marcelle, one of my father's older sisters, married another teacher, Paul, and they asked to be moved to the same little town, really a big market village, Taourirt. We dwelt in small cottages among the whitewashed, mostly one-roomed, but clean and flat-roofed houses of the Arabs. We always said "Arabs", and I will continue to do so for the sake of simplification, but I believe that most people around us were Shluhs, the indigenous Africans, a race very close to that of Saint Augustine but converted to Islam, while keeping some particular traditions. They were of light brown complexion, of independent character and dignified. They wore woolen *burnouses* (large, long cloaks with a hood). Most women were unveiled and jewelled. Even the poor wore silver ornaments and painted their faces and hands with ochre henna. The rich ones had gold, amber and amethyst or turquoise on their heads, ears, necks, arms and ankles, and they were heavily veiled, often leaving only a small triangle of their face free from their embroidered masks, so as to see their way with a single eye. Soon I was speaking Arabic with our maids and neighbors.

This part of Morocco, far from the sea, has an extreme tropical climate. It could hardly be cultivated (some progress has been made with irrigation), but some sheep grazed on the short, hard grass of the plains. It was stifling hot during the long summer, and around midnight people used to gather near the road from Oujda, waiting for a truck that brought big blocks of ice from this bigger frontier city. There was no electricity yet at Tauorirt, though some generator must have been installed soon after our arrival, as we had even a kind of unpredictable cinema. I have a general impression of glaring light, oppressive heat, harshness and solitude, without precise memories of people or places.

This recently colonized Moroccan frontier was a kind of African "Far West". One of the Europeans was always playing with a loaded shotgun when he took a walk, killing any animal in view, even domesticated dogs. At four, when I could discern cruelty more clearly, I hated him. He ended by killing a man while playing poker, and my father was witness when he was judged and condemned. Another one used to nail crowds of living animals to the walls of his own house, inside and outside the rooms, and he was able to live and sleep with all that agony around him. He sold the skins, saying that the quality was better when the animals died slowly. I am sure he was responsible for the nightmares I often had.

In the bars when someone did not have the right amount of money, the barmen cut the notes in two instead of making change. It obliged the customers to come back, as they could do nothing with half a note. There were many strange customs like this.

From 11 A.M. to 4 P.M., life seemed to stop, as everybody had to take refuge in some shade, preferably between the thick mud walls of a house, to escape the burning heat. There was always unrest among the tribes of the nearby Atlas mountains. Sometimes trains of wounded soldiers stopped at the little station of Taourirt. My mother had compassion on them and gave them food and drink. She used to bring fruits, eggs and small aluminum plates to the wagons. It was so hot at the unroofed station that she had only to break the eggs in the metal plates and to place them on the rails. A few minutes later all the eggs were fried. She was, without knowing it, a pioneer in the use of solar energy.

Life had its dangers. There was no hospital or clinic nearby or in the town, though there was a school where my father worked with competence and youthful enthusiasm. The plain was covered with stones, and scorpions hid under most of the biggest ones. There were myriads of mosquitoes, biting flies and other harmful insects and, of course, venomous serpents. I have been told that one day my uncle heard me call joyfully, "Tonton Paul, come and see the beautiful ribbon." He peeped out at the courtyard and saw his small niece, two and a half years old, with a large pink ribbon like a giant butterfly in her hair, fondly patting another "ribbon" ornamented with regular patterns: an exceptionally large adder. The snake looked quite tolerant, if not grateful (who can know?), for the caress, but my uncle was frozen with fear. He shook himself and jumped into the house to fetch a gun. He tried to steady his hand, as he had to avoid harming me and provoking the serpent. He was a good marksman, fortunately, and blew off the snake's head, which made me cry and mourn the whole day.

My Uncle Paul and Aunt Marcelle were with us; Paul Texier, a Vendean, met my father's sister, Marcelle, at a teachers' conference. They eventually married, and my uncle applied for a teaching appointment at Taourirt. Given the charms of the place, it was not usually sought after by young teachers, and his request was granted. So it happened that we were five Bretons of the same family under this fierce sun: soon six, when my cousin, Paul (Paulo as a child), was born. When we left Taourirt for Safi, my uncle did the same. When we moved to Casablanca, we were separated for a time because he was less qualified than my father. But finally they were again close to us. My cousin, Paulo, also an only child and two years younger than I, became like a brother to me. My uncle was a perfect atheist and a "venerable" in a masonic lodge. Paul was never baptized. I was fond of my cousin, who was an intelligent and sensitive boy.

As I was a precocious child, in my early years my parents were usually proud of me. My mother wanted me to be pretty like her, and I responded with some success, though with no more than ordinary achievements later on; and I felt an almost complete indifference in matters of clothing. This was to be one of our areas of disagreement. My father wanted me to be exceptionally intelligent and even intellectual like himself, and he helped me to acquire more knowledge and sophistication than was good for my years. Before I was three years old, I knew my letters well and was soon reading with eagerness and illusions of understanding the left-wing newspapers and political reviews that were always scattered in our home. I was very lively in spite of the harsh climate, curious and self-willed. My parents never slapped or beat me. I believe it was against their principles. But they showed annoyance at my fancies and tempers in such a way that I was convinced they did not love me. They always treated me as far more mature than I could reasonably be, and, because my mind could meet the challenge, they never realized that affectively I was still a child. Of course I could not analyze this, but I suffered from it deeply until my adolescence. I still responded to my father's teaching, but I developed a constant though low-level conflict with my mother. Avoiding contact with her, who was a normal, often pleasant young woman, though sometimes aggressive when frustrated and unable to understand or reach me, I turned more and more to my father, his ideas and his books. Soon the other children ceased to interest me. Those of my own age did not relish intellectual exploration; the older ones rejected me because I was much younger and more advanced in studies. This was to continue for years. Without understanding why, I was conscious of a weight upon me and of constant loneliness.

At this time in my story, when I was three years old, something happened inside and outside me that I remember vividly with all its particular circumstances as if it stood out sharply against the grey background of half-forgotten memories. Along with my Baptism, this experience was to be the source of my whole spiritual life.

We had had several days of *sirocco*. It was not a rare occurrence but always a trying one. This strong, burning wind from the Sahara desert carries northward thousands of tons of red, finely ground sand into the open plains. Even the Arabs were rarely seen outside when it blew, and then only wrapped tightly in their *burnouses*, which were often blown from them, as were their roofs and their sheep. No schools, no stores, no bars were open. If someone touched a piece of metal or even wood outside the house, his skin would remain on the object. Even with drawn curtains, locked shutters and windows framed in cotton or wool, everything in our rooms was still covered or filled with sand. We ate it, breathed it, were powdered or whipped by it. We had the choice of being steamed inside or roasted outside.

Suddenly the wind abated in the afternoon. Even the forgotten silence felt cool. People went out of their homes immediately to breathe freely and to assess the wind's mischief around them. Our maid took me out in the evening. She sat me on a small mat, enjoining me to remain there. This I did, too tired to disobey.

Suddenly the sky over me and in some way around me, as I was on a small hillock, was all afire. The glory of the sunset was perhaps reflected in the myriads of particles of powdery sand still floating in the air. It was like an immense, feathery flame all scarlet from one pole to the other, with touches of crimson and, on one side, of deep purple. I was caught in limitless beauty and radiant, singing splendor. And at the same time, with a cry of wonder in my heart, I *knew* that all this beauty was created, I knew GOD. This was the word that my parents had hidden from me. I had nothing to name him: God, Dieu, Allah or Yahweh, as he is named by human lips, but my heart knew that *all was from him* and him alone and that he was such that I could address him and enter into relationship with him through prayer. I made my first act of adoration.

This does appear dramatic. It was. And after more than sixty years, it is still in me. Not once could I dismiss this experience, whatever my intellectual doubts might have been in the following years. This act of adoration was not to be isolated. I began then a life of prayer. I tried to say something of it to my father, but he did not understand at all. If only I had known the noun, God. It was probably better that he did not understand, though I found myself more alone than ever, with an essential part of myself and my life incommunicable and unshared for many years. But I held to it because I sensed that it was infinitely precious.

Everything afterward is just confused memories: markets under the lattice roofs that sheltered the sheep, the baskets of figs and oranges or the earthen jars with patches of light and shade, our walks in the evening with a tame chameleon on our shoulders to rid us of bothersome insects, and the nights when I knelt down near my bed. I had never seen anybody kneel down in worship, but there was an instinct telling me to do so and, in the morning, to offer the day to the unnamed One who had created me and all beauty, all goodness, all being in the universe.

Chapter III

Safi

We moved to Safi, a sparkling, small, white city on the shores of the ocean, "my ocean", the Atlantic. I had never seen it, except perhaps as an infant at Brest. But as soon as I saw, heard, smelled and touched "her", I knew that this was my mother, just as the descendants of generations of peasants recognize Mother Earth. I was fascinated by the changing hues of her waves, by the mysterious depths of her salty waters and by the way she meets with the sky and hides innumerable forms of life in her moving tides. I was attuned to her song even when her waves came crashing thunderously on the rocks, and her immensity was not frightening to me but soothing and embracing. I was not, however, to have a full relationship with her at Safi. Instead I came to love the diversity of Africa with her many lands, peoples and cultures.

The climate of the region was mild, thanks to the ocean breeze, and our house was comfortable. I think that my parents were happy, as they met other young couples, had interesting work and went to many parties, dances and *soirées*. But they were not very discerning in their choice of friends. Morocco was still a land full of promise for adventurers and soldiers of fortune. So it happened that one of our neighbors (we had flats in the same building) was a real bandit. Thomas was an attractive young man with fair hair and laughing eyes. He was so tall and strong that, when he invited my mother to dance, she complained that her feet never touched the floor. He was supposed to be in the sheep market or something like that, but his real business was negotiating big insurance policies on cars and having them wrecked without harm to himself or his customers. The scheme was to be his ruin, because he also tried his hand at small planes later on, and through some error he was himself killed in an aircraft he had ordered to be crashed.

While he was our friend, however, he looked respectable enough, and he took much interest in me, as I did in him. He probably saw that I had some ability and a natural taste for gangster life, and he undertook my training as at least a promising little thief. My parents were totally unaware of what was going on. This was part of my sworn alliance with Thomas and part of the fun. I remember only in general all the exercises I had to perform, except those I continued after he left us. I became very good at picking locks. I lost the skill only after long years of monastic life, due to a lack of opportunity. I recall clearly that one day I had a great disappointment. Thomas knew that I was fond of *couscous*, a North African dish of steamed wheat and thick, spiced soup. He told me that he would invite me to a delicious *couscous* if I succeeded in stealing the silver spoons that were normally locked in a special cupboard in our dining room. Two days later I went triumphantly to my "boss" with the silver, but he withdrew my reward because I had not thought to choose a day when my mother would be long in noticing the theft. Such was my training.

At the same time that I was pursuing these side activities, my father was feeding my five-year-old mind with revolutionary pamphlets and explaining that "*la propriété c'est le vol*"

("Property is theft") (Proud'hon). "The real thieves are those who own what should belong to all. Everything belongs to whoever needs it." He was a great defender of the *reprise individuelle* as a preparation for the revolution that would cure all the injustices of the world. The strange thing is that my father himself (he had had, after all, a Christian upbringing) was scrupulously honest, to the point of paying for my own pencils and copybooks while he was distributing the government supplies to other pupils free of charge. I did feel confused among all these adult contradictions and did not make much of the current standard of morality.

I was particularly bewildered in the following circumstances: I had been storing sugar under my toys for my favorite dog-friend. When he visited us, accompanied by his master (this is how I saw the hierarchy), I fed him with several lumps at once; but the wretched animal escaped my hands and bounced back happily into the drawing room with its mouth still filled with sugar, wagging its tail. I was punished for hoarding this commodity "unlawfully removed" from the kitchen cupboard. I could not figure out what law this violated or why I should not apply my father's principles and Thomas' example.

In fact, I did not see at all why I should obey my parents and not my parents obey me, when I felt that I had often such better judgment (though I would concede that my father was sometimes worth listening to).

It was not quite the same with lying. I loved truth and had an instinct for its value. But lying was poetic and practical, and everybody lied more or less. So I lied with remorse or said the truth regretfully and was never in peace.

No one had any idea of these inner conflicts. No one knew that I was continuing to kneel down every day and say to the God of my heart that I was adoring him, believing him, loving him but that life was a complicated affair for a five-year-old torn between what she did not know was his voice in her, her conscience's call, and so many opposed but attractive appeals within and without her. There was no way I could talk about this or even find someone to talk to.

School was very boring. When I was not interested in a subject, I refused to learn and was scolded. When it was interesting, I wanted to know everything about it, and the other pupils did not follow, so the teacher was annoyed. I decided to end my days of schooling progressively. In the morning my mother kissed me goodbye, and sometimes her eyes followed me as far as the curve of the short road to school. After that I was on my own. I had only to take another turn and walk rapidly on small paths through the fields to reach a pasture land, where I could hide behind crumbling stone walls, surrounded by objects at least worth studying: the asphodels, those pink wildflowers taller than myself, light, straight and dancing in the wind, the jewelled beetles, some painted with yellow dots or orange backs, some graced with lustrous blue wings, the thick cacti and the short brown grass that the sheep were cropping close to the soil. I wondered how the sheep could make wool with brown grass and why the butterflies were so hesitant in their flights and never looked satisfied with the flowers. These were far more important questions than those about letters and numbers that were continually asked at school.

Before midday I returned home, careful to avoid the sun because it burned my eyes. I suffered much from an eye disease that some time before had almost destroyed my sight. It might have been trachoma, which was endemic in Morocco, and the pain lasted for several years. This helped me to be believed when, several days each month, after playing truant, I told my teachers that my mother had kept me home. But the extra holidays were doomed to be discovered and were. Then I had to go to school every day, ignominiously accompanied to the very door. And I spent the tedious hours, sometimes dreaming, sometimes organizing breaches of discipline and sometimes reading adventure books concealed under my desk. I had no friend there. The little girls with dolls irritated me, and the boys were unfriendly, though I found them more interesting, and I liked marbles. However I still loved my cousin, Paulo, and talked or played with him. I did so, too, with a nine-year-old Jewish neighbor.

Sarah lived with her large, well-to-do family. They were all strictly observant Pharisees. In the Moroccan towns there were often groups of Jews who had lived there for centuries, preserving their own way of life in the midst of Moslems and, recently, of Christians. In their synagogues you could find the Torah, the Talmud and other venerated commentaries of the Law written in a way that showed the evolution of letters and of their support through the ages: the rolls of pressed skins, the parchments, the papyri, the Eastern paper and the modern sheets. There were both Moslems and Jews in our predominantly French school. French people did not believe in apartheid. Strange to say, only the private Catholic schools were not integrated, with the rare exceptions of very rich students from the Arab masculine elite. Sarah was a thoughtful and, for her age, well-read girl. She never spoke of religion, though it had much place in her family life, but one day she told me: "My parents do not want me to stay with you because you are only an atheist." I was hurt by the scorn in her tone, and I answered, maybe with one of my father's sentences: "What of that? It is certainly more intelligent than believing in God or in *djinns*" (the spirits that superstitious Moslem women used to see everywhere). It was her turn to be hurt, and though we still played and chatted together quite often, we never went back to the subject. But how I cried! I felt that I had betrayed more than my own soul, and I learned the prayer of contrition.

Some months after that, on a Jewish feast, Sarah's parents sent us a large cake on a rich plate. Safi was famous for blue ceramics. When touched by metal, the vessels made in this town sounded like silver bells, and the plates were artistically decorated with complex arabesques in brown, yellow and black with a predominant vivid blue. We ate the cake and returned the plate with thanks. The day after, my mother found it on our threshold, broken into pieces. She asked for an explanation, and Sarah's mother said that we should never have washed her plate with ours, because sometimes, perhaps this very day, we might have been eating pork. As good Pharisees, they would not have their plates contaminated by water that had perhaps touched pork. It was the end of our relationship. Fanaticism was expressed in a far worse way some years after this incident, when one of our friends snatched, barely in time, a baby from surrounding flames. His mother was screaming nearby but did not make a gesture to save her own son for fear of touching fire on a Sabbath day when cooking is forbidden. When we had a Jewish maid, she could not switch the electricity on or off on Saturdays. My father observed that the stupidity of all religious people could not be matched by anything save their unkindness and pride. I stored this judgment in my growing treasure of contradictory aphorisms.

To my parents, their small daughter was a source of innumerable problems of practical education. My father, a very successful teacher at school, was often at a loss at home when dealing with my stubbornness, tempers, laziness and other faults. I don't think I was really lazy, however; and I even put unexpected energy into a number of tasks. But I wanted to choose them, and my choices were not those of my parents most of the time. I will give only one example in some detail; it may be better than several concise ones mentioned only in passing.

My parents were planning a family celebration for the sixth anniversary of their marriage. I was told its meaning and approved of it, especially as cherries, my favorite fruit, were to be the dessert. My mother went to buy them at the nearby market, and I made a careful exploration of the kitchen during her absence. The meal had been prepared already, and there was a plateful of giant shrimps (a rare delicacy from the ocean), freshly boiled and waiting for seasoning under a white cloth. I went to the balcony of the house, which had two stories, and I looked down on the street. Just in front of our door an Arab boy was searching for lice under his clothes, which were little more than rags and strings. I thought that he would be pleased with a big shrimp. I fetched one and threw it on his head. Well, he was certainly pleased. He ate it on the spot and asked for more. I obliged. I don't know how it happened, but when I came back from the kitchen there were three urchins with expectant faces at our door. So I took the plate and continued to throw down the fat, pink shrimps, one by one, from the balcony. Soon there was a happy little crowd, fighting, laughing and looking up at me. In the middle of this success came mother. When she saw what the commotion was about, she called sternly: "Lucette, stop immediately!" I saw that time was short and threw the few remaining shrimps all at once to the eager company below. Fate decreed that the last one should fall into the basket of cherries. It did not cheer my mother but may have given her an idea for the penance that, after consulting my father, she gave me: I was not to taste the cherries, not even one! I did not complain. We ate our meal without shrimps, and then the fruit disappeared under my serene eyes. I certainly did not show any unbecoming longing while my parents were mournfully eating the shiny red fruit that they wished so much to share with me. But they had to do their duty as educators. And when it was all finished, they heard the calm voice of their little daughter asking: "Is not Lucette very, very kind? She has left *all* the cherries for Dad and Mama!" Having the last word was well worth losing some cherries.

I don't know if it was because I was unsatisfactory in obedience or in health that the following year it was decided to send me to France for some time. God prepared me for the journey.

It was Sunday. I was bored and in search of new ways of entertaining myself. Mother wanted to chat with a friend and handed me a big book. She may have said: "Take this and be quiet. There are lots of nice pictures there." I sat on the thick, rust-colored carpet and examined the book. I can still see it clearly. It was a very fat book, though what looked big at that age would perhaps not seem so now. It was only a catalogue of some Parisian stores, the "Samaritaine" or "Galeries la Fayette", with a thousand items listed and illustrated. They could be mailed to you if you sent the money. I did not know that, but I liked the variety of the small pictures showing dresses, bottles of perfume, hats, lamps, pieces of furniture, clocks. And there, in the right-hand corner of one page, I saw three crosses of different designs, each one with a tiny man on it and some numbers underneath. I had never seen a crucifix, only sometimes a cross, which had no meaning for me, on top of a building called a "church", which was for "the meetings of superstitious people". But while I was silently looking at these strange pictures, I suddenly *knew*: this man on the cross had been killed, and it was for all

men, women and children. It was for me. He was a man, but
he was also the Son of the God whom I was already adoring
as Creator and loving, universal presence. He was God. I
would not have formulated this in one sentence as I do now,
but all this was gathered in one insight and clearly formed
even with words in my mind, contrary to my first "sunset"
religious experience, which had been purely intuitive. It is
very difficult to explain, because this complex theology was
taught to me in a moment and looked perfectly simple and
as evident as a first principle, given as absolute truth. It also
looked perfectly normal.

My Baptism was bearing fruit in circumstances when the
usual transmission of faith was impossible. My mind would
one day be so filled with atheistic propaganda that I would
be unable to believe in Christ intellectually; but, deeper than
the thoughts of men, the thoughts of the Spirit had been
imprinted in me. Even if I could not understand it or accept
it logically, I was obliged to acknowledge that Jesus was the
Son of God and was God, Man and Savior. I could not even
have an existential doubt about it. I have always known it in
all certitude, though limitedly, and been conscious that God
himself was the only source of this knowledge.

Hope also took on a new dimension in me, and my heart
opened to the love of the crucified Lord. I kissed the picture
of the bigger crucifix (hardly three centimeters long) and
tore it off swiftly, taking care not to be heard. Then I
searched for a hiding place. I still had a baby toy, a small
shaker, which had not been discarded when I began to walk
because it was silver. I inserted the bit of paper into it
through a slit. This was my prize, my treasure, my secret
icon! It was never to be discovered. The paper was fortunately quite strong, but the day came when it was finally
worn out from being so often taken out of its hiding place

by loving fingers, contemplated with wondering eyes and kissed by a small child's lips.

All this did not prevent me from being a trouble to my inexperienced parents. They may also have expressed a concern about my health to Aunt Jeanne (I will say "Tante Jeanne", as we called her), who proposed to take me with her for one year. This was gratefully accepted, and off I went with a lady friend, crying for my father but consoled by the thought of being for a long time on the ocean in a big boat. A huge teddy bear and a small silver shaker accompanied me.

Chapter IV

Back to Brittany

My grandparents (on my father's side) were delighted to see me, at least for a time. After I had tried a knife on the carvings of the unused dining room to improve the shape of a tree, escaped several times into the streets, suffocated myself in an attempt to climb inside the chimney and other such daily entertainments, they were not too sad to see me off with Tante Jeanne. There were certainly fewer apples, pears and gooseberries in the garden after two weeks than when I had arrived, and grandmother was a little tired of cooking chicken, because I told her that it was the staple food in Morocco (which was quite untrue) and that I could not live without a tender wing at each lunch.

But I had a more serious question to ask: given the rare honor of entering her bedroom, I saw a crucifix standing on a mahogany set of drawers between two big seashells. I so longed to know about him and above all his Name! I pointed at him: "Grandma, who is he?" She sighed and took my hand in hers. "My little one, I cannot tell you." "Why? Tell me now. Please, tell me!" I was almost crying, but she answered me sadly, "No, I promised your father that I would never tell you about him; and if we speak of him, your father will never see me again." I was silent. This One on the Cross I loved above everything else. But, next to him, I cherished and trusted my father. Could they be antagonists? I felt once more torn and paralyzed.

Before I left Brest I returned for an unallowed and solitary visit to the crucifix. I examined it closely. There was something written on it: INRI (the initials of *Jesus Nazarenus Rex Iudeorum*). I repeated, "Inri. . . . Inri. . . ." Can it be his name? I tried it, but somehow it did not feel right, though I sometimes used it until, two years later, I learned at last that his name was JESUS.

Then another idea came: What about an exploration of Little Marie's room? No one but she ever entered there. Thanks to Thomas' training, but with a racing heart, I unlocked the door, though the lock was above my head, and I entered. It was more like a large cupboard than a room: just enough place for a narrow, iron bed with a spotless eiderdown, a shelf on which to hang clothing and a very small table with a basin and a blue enamel jug. There is great poverty here, I thought; there is peace. I feel well. Let us see what is in the pocket of Marie's Sunday dress: a few pennies and some printed pages in Breton. Some paper images like the ones on the wall. This one near the bed is not unpleasant: a lady with a blue veil. Something is written in French: *"Marie des Sources"* (Mary of the Springs). It is a nice name. Can the lady be a relative of Little Marie? No, she is too pretty and refined. Something fills my heart, and again I know: she is the Mother of the Crucified One. I still do not know his name, but now I know hers; it is written: Mary! A noise downstairs. Quickly I shut the door and run down the steps. During the evening meal I look at the maid who brings the soup. She usually sits down with us at the table but remains silent. Perhaps she will explain one day what I want to understand? Perhaps she will tell me the Name? No, my father would never come to see her again, and she would be so sad. Everybody loves my father, and he makes them do what he wants. How can I love and be free? Grandmother smiles at me. She may be thinking that I dream of Morocco.

I slept downstairs, and, every evening after grandmother had kissed me and smoothed my sheets, she climbed up the stairs to her room. I waited a little, put on the lights again and read grandfather's newspapers. Not this night. I was too busy thinking big thoughts. And I remember them very well. I repeated, "Mary is his Mother." Like everything that I knew this way, it seemed evident, normal and matter-of-fact. I did not wonder how a woman could be Mother of God. It looked perfectly sure and fitting. But this time I had some problems related to it. Was she *my* mother, too? Could I address her as "Mama"? This was a good question. Its answer would solve all my problems. So I said to God: "Please," (I was always polite when I spoke to him) "if I may call your mother 'Mama', just make me see it. I will count up to three; at three exactly, put off the light." It was a miracle I wanted, though a small one. The switch was near the door, far from my bed. I counted: "One—two—three." At that exact moment, darkness enveloped me, and grandmother's voice said, "Don't keep the electricity on. You should be asleep by now." I felt bewildered. "What should I believe? Is it God who switched off the light, or is it grandmother? May I call Mary 'Mama' or not?" Then there was a little interior light. It was difficult. I struggled and caught it: it was God through grandmother who had acted. He had used her. He could do anything. But what was his own part in each event? I was discovering secondary causes, but with a sense of ambiguity. I would call Mary "Mama", but never again would I ask for direct divine intervention. Two years later, when I was eight or nine, my father gave me some books of philosophy, and I understood far more than he had expected. I was no genius, but I had already thought many thoughts bigger than my child's head.

It was often tiring and lonely, however, and, now for a time, to be forgotten. During the whole year I spent with Tante Jeanne, I was a child among children, treated as such, loved as such, happy and carefree as such. I don't think I could have become a fully normal person without this short but intense period of real childhood that took place at Camaret.

Chapter V

Camaret

Camaret is a big fishing village with few "strangers" (meaning persons from other parts of France), situated at the very tip of Europe. We used to say "at the tip of the world", where land ends and an almost infinite expanse of water begins. Our school on the cliff was surrounded by the ocean on three sides, with enormous rocks carved and cragged by the relentless effort of monstrous waves, boulders projected by the thousands to the land after having been smoothed against the reefs by centuries of shocks and grinding, and subterranean caves that could be reached only at low tides and sparkled when the sunset briefly touched their walls of rock crystal. There was no sound other than the sharp calls of gulls and the roaring of the sea, swelling during the tempests, abating when the wind died down, but always present. The ocean is rarely gentle in these rough surroundings; each deep wave crashes, foams and recedes, and another one comes swiftly. Treacherous currents have to be avoided by sailors. Not far from there, the "Bay of the Dead" (*Baie des Trépassés*) opens its mournful arms; there the sea brought back those she had killed afar. It does not happen often in our days of safer journeys and bigger boats. I loved this sealand with passion as soon as I saw the gulls diving in its tormented waters and the red sails in a haze of glory at sunrise.

Tante Jeanne would never let me swim, but everything there was ocean or from the ocean. The clouds looked like part of it; it made the air salty; it had shaped the islands in front of us and also the race of obstinate, taciturn, courageous people who lived in the slate-roofed cottages of grey granite, on the dunes covered with purple briars or around the chapel of Rocamadour, down at the quay. This church was witness to the centuries of ardent faith that my Celtic ancestors had lived and preserved, but I never entered it.

My private kingdom was to be the school where my aunt had her home with two other unmarried teachers. Each one had a separate, large room with a kitchen and a kind of common hall. Before 1930, there was not even electricity in this isolated "end of the world" village; but the soft light of our big lamps was both bright and intimate. Not far from us lived the Breton poet called St. Pol, and in a nearby creek we could visit a famous boat, a pioneer of the North Pole exploration. She had known many thrilling adventures with her captain Charcot and had a name worthy of him: "The Why Not?" ("*le Pourquoi pas?*"). It made me dream heroic dreams.

The school looked big to me, but I guess that with only three teachers it was indeed quite a small girls' primary school. Each class had two or three divisions corresponding to grades; and the teachers were kept busy going from one group to the other, keeping discipline and preventing the pupils from speaking Breton or from sleeping on their desks, as some of them had heavy tasks to perform before school began. Many were still wearing *sabots* (wooden shoes). Though I knew so much more than all my companions and was the niece of the teacher, I never felt superior to them; I never labeled them stupid, ignorant or boring, as I had done the other children in Morocco. I enjoyed being, playing and talking with them. I was one of them. This year was for me a year of healing and happiness in sound surroundings. Most of the credit was due to Tante Jeanne.

Christians are wont to think that nobody can be fully selfless, loving, sincere, and so on without worshipping in their Church. When I began to mingle with Catholics, this arrogance surprised me very much. My dear father had totally ruined the faith and Christian hope of Tante Jeanne. She had an extreme admiration for her bright young brother and was soon convinced of the truth of his apostolic atheism and of his grievances against a religion of "bourgeois oppressors and warmongers". For her, war and exploitation of the poor were the ultimate evils; and she deplored a Church so commonly on the side of the rich and the military. It looked a little simplistic, but it was easy to back this opinion with a multitude of historical facts and examples. Besides, who could still believe in all those myths: creation in seven days, a God made man, and ascension into heaven? We were in an enlightened century.

Tante Jeanne was nervous, plain, still unmarried (she was close to forty when she astonished us all by her wedding) and considered a good teacher, though far from my father's sparkling performances. But she was goodness itself. She had treasures of kindness for anybody in need of them. She practiced forgetfulness of self to heroic extremes; and, never having read spiritual books or attempted introspection, she was completely unaware of her virtues and blissfully free from any temptation to self-admiration or self-pity. She could have been bitter if she had considered how often her kindness was abused and how little rewarded, but kindness was her very nature, and she was so busy working for others' happiness that she could not think of her own. I took it for granted that she was at my service; and I warmed myself by her love, profited from her discreet activity, expected her to sacrifice herself to my needs and fancies, without thinking any more than anyone else (or even she herself) did that she was more to be thanked for than the sun on our faces.

Somehow though, I was learning that generosity, tenderness and care were dimensions of eternal love. It was obvious to me that this eternal love that had often touched me with its light and warmth was inhabiting Tante Jeanne's heart and life, no matter what her borrowed agnosticism made her think or say. One day I was to read, "God is love, and anyone who lives in love lives in God and God in him" (Jn 4:16). Tante Jeanne never referred to any religious subject with me nor I with her. My only danger with her was to become a spoiled child, but even this was not likely. She brought herself sometimes to be firm for the sake of my improvement. Though I did cry over the multiplication tables, I had to memorize them; and though I had no love for water in winter, I had to wash. These were my only hardships during my eleven and a half months of childhood.

Joy, wonder and enthusiastic activities filled my days. Some of my many discoveries, however, were accompanied by disappointment. The first snows made me dizzy with exultation. I could not stop dancing my praise for this soft, scintillating, feathery creature coming from the skies. When the bell rang for our grammar class, I poured an apronful of it onto my desk so that I could at least look at it from time to time during the lessons. There was a big stove in the room. Water soon ran on my knees, colored with the blue ink from my copybooks. I needed much consolation after such a betrayal from usually kind Nature. At the same period, cunning violence shocked me even more. During the brief snow season, we often met with the pupils of the neighboring boys' school for a friendly snowball battle. One day a boy concealed a stone in a snowball and hit one of my friends on the head. She fell bleeding and almost unconscious at my side. I distrusted boys ever after that. We played almost always without toys, though some girls had dolls. I was always ready to give mine away. We liked fairy stories and were proud of cultivating our tiny gardens of hollyhocks and larkspurs all around the schoolyard or looking after fluffy chickens, or just jumping and running and laughing in the fresh wind. We never talked of anything much outside our little world of playmates, family events, animals or sea and the funny side of adults, especially our teachers.

Once only, one of the older girls (she must have been almost ten) asked me, "Do you have an angel, even though you do not go to Mass?" I must have looked puzzled, because she added this piece of information about angels: "They are small men with wings, and they protect us." Then again a ray of a different kind of light visited me, and I answered with full assurance, "Angels are not little men. They have no bodies, and they help us to see God." She laughed at me: "Do you see God?" I replied honestly, "No." And that was all. I was annoyed and confused because I had not expressed properly my sudden faith in the existence of radiant spirits who were interested in our spiritual welfare. I added this to my collection of theological tidbits. They were really no more than islands in a sea of ignorance, but very beautiful, solid islands, and they made sense to me. However, angels never entered my life as the Lord himself or even Mary had done. I am afraid that the small rabbits that had just been bought to be raised in the school were the source of more wonder to me at the time than all the angels of heaven. But I never forgot to pray secretly to God, morning and evening and whenever I was moved to admiration or compassion, which was often.

Tante Jeanne was very nervous when "*M. l'Inspecteur*" was supposed to come. We pupils were merely excited when all kinds of rehearsals, examinations, cleaning and singing were added to our light schedules. I say singing because the Breton accent transforms the French into a tone language, and everything we recited together was like a song. The inspector came and he was big and stern. Tante Jeanne in her shyness lost some of her easy skill with children when she gave her lessons under his scrutiny, but as a whole it went rather well. She offered him a drink in her own apartment after the classes, and he accepted. She brought a small bottle of expensive liquor reserved for special guests. The inspector swallowed the content of a short glass in one gulp, coughed in a large handkerchief and hurried away. The two other teachers came down immediately to discuss their performance. Tante Jeanne said:

"At first he looked satisfied, but maybe he is unwell. He looked annoyed at the end."

"What do you mean by 'at the end'?"

"Well, just now after his drink."

Miss Fer, the older teacher, drew the bottle to herself, uncorked it and cried out, "Jeanne, what have you done? Is this not the strong vinegar that you bought to clean the furred tiles of your kitchen?"

It was.

I have many other remembrances of this happy year, but they would take many pages, and we still have a long way to go.

It all ended with our holidays in Vendée, a province south of Brittany, home of my Uncle Paul. The orchards were gorgeous that year. There were so many peaches, plums, and pears that the farmers had no objection to our band of ten or twelve children eating as much fruit as we wanted. We ate them on the trees and under the trees, ripe, unripe and overripe. We often got sick but enjoyed ourselves thoroughly. But one day I tried to pat a beautiful, golden, furry bee and was stung. I did not mind so much the swollen finger as the pain of misunderstood intentions. I must honestly recall that, according to my uncle, I led the band of "more or less cousins" through creative behavior into a series of catastrophes and that, consequently, Tante Jeanne was more exhausted after than before the holidays. If so, I did not intend it. In fact, I tried to make myself useful in the house, in the awkward manner of small children.

This was because of a short conversation I had had with Tante Jeanne before we left Camaret. One Sunday when, as was not usually the case, we were home, I was awakened early by birds celebrating the dawn in a climbing rose tree that framed our window with pink blossoms. I was in a very large bed that I shared with Tante Jeanne. I tried to push her out of its warmth because I wanted my coffee, and I also clamored for a new book that she must fetch me from the attic. She mildly protested, "It is not even six o'clock. Let me sleep!" I answered indignantly, "How can you sleep when I want a book?" She looked at me with a smile and argued back, "And how can you want a book so early when I need rest?" Even as she was saying that, she jumped from the bed and went to the attic with a coat over her nightgown. My own selfishness was revealed to me that day, and I asked to help sweep the floor of my beloved slave. Grandmother was glad when I offered to set the table and hull the peas during the last days of my stay in Brittany. She did not know that I would soon lose my good will in other surroundings, and she said: "You are growing; your mother will be very happy."

The same day she took me apart, gave me some oval, smooth sweets and told me, "My little one, those sugar almonds are from your Baptism feast. I have kept them for you until now. Eat them, but above all remember that you have been baptized. It is important that you know it." I did not understand, but I could not forget her words because there were tears in her eyes. I did not tell anybody either about what I sensed was a secret between us, a happy secret in spite of the tears.

Chapter VI

Casablanca

My parents had moved to Casablanca, which is the largest city in Morocco, though Rabat is the administrative capital. Casablanca means "White Dwelling", and the ocean mirrors its multitude of small, terraced, whitewashed houses and its high-rise modern buildings.

My parents were eagerly waiting for me, but something went wrong immediately. They had sent to France a graceful little girl, pale and rather serious, whom they had seen growing quick-witted and precocious. And here, coming back to them, was a perfect stranger, a miniature Breton peasant, with cheeks round and red like apples (I was to lose them very quickly), a singsong accent and a screaming yellow coat, which made her complexion even more startling under the African sun. My mother was horrified. I saw it and withdrew from her first kiss. She then made some disparaging remarks to my father about Tante Jeanne's taste in choosing the yellow coat, and it infuriated me. My father was bewildered, too, because in just one year I had grown so different from what he remembered; but he was less outgoing and did not say anything. I did not feel welcome. I hated the harsh sun and the noisy streets. By the time I was in our flat, the festival meal had no meaning, and I refused to eat it. My mother, who had spent the whole morning preparing it, was soon reduced to tears. She said that I was unpleasant on purpose. Then began a series of deeply painful misunderstandings. They were to last for years.

After a stay in a Spanish suburb, I was enrolled in the biggest school in the city, with pupils from first to twelfth grade, a mixture of Arab, Jew, Central-European, Greek, Spanish, Maltese girls (and boys on the other side) with a few French children. I was then seven and was to spend a year in a class of twelve- or thirteen-year-old city children of uprooted families, many of them very depraved. I will not try to describe the kind of games they played or the conditions laid down to enter their little bands. I knew that I could not touch that. I was repelled and threatened, but I could not speak of it. My father was one day to become the principal of this school and helped to cleanse it of the coarsest immoralities, but at that time he was unaware that the school was a center of many youthful vices. Most of the children were poor, and hygiene was unknown in their families. I had only one friend, again a Jewish girl. She was very greedy and robbed me of a gold bracelet. Such jewels were worn even by young girls in Morocco. I pretended that I did not know who had stolen it. But she was still a child in other ways, as I was. We managed to remain so in the midst of constant moral dangers, pressures and loathsome examples.

It was then that the country suffered a major locust plague. One day, in midmorning when we were at recreation, we heard a confusion of noises from different parts of the city. People were beating drums, pans and scraps of iron, shouting and whistling. Suddenly what seemed to be an enormous cloud came rapidly toward us. It was becoming larger and denser so swiftly that soon the sun was obscured. A strange, dim light came through the millions of wings that were beating in the uncanny cloud. It arrived above us, and it became almost night. Then it descended, and we could see the first insects, as long as my hand or an adult's forefinger, dropping on our heads and shoulders, on the tarred floor of the courtyard, on the trees and windowsills, on every inch of ground for miles and miles. They were big, ugly and clutching, already devouring every bit of leaf, bark or grass in view. Not only was everything covered by their green and yellow bodies but they were tearing at our shirts, climbing up our knees or down our sleeves—and biting! (In fact the scratching was done by the toothed legs.) Many teachers and most of the pupils were terrified. I was both curious and repelled.

It was difficult to get home. We were living in a fifth-floor apartment with a terrace, and there, too, it was full of locusts. Our cat, who had begun to catch and eat some of them, went mad when a heap of insects were trapped in her fur and she saw more crowds toppling on her. My parents had a small car, and we tried to get out of the city the following Sunday, but it was impossible. Not only were the wheels glued in the mass of killed insects, but thousands of them were still on the wing, hitting the wind-screen, which was soon opaque with their blood. It was horrible. The Arabs, after looking at their devastated fields, were filling sacks with the culprits and roasting them. I was too young to make economic evaluations, but my father became very busy with projects for feeding starving children not only that year but the following one, when the crickets born of the invasion again devoured whatever could grow on the shorn land.

As my father was thus more and more involved in political and relief activities and my mother was working in transmission, I was often alone at home and did whatever pleased me. Most often I read adult books or went on forbidden explorations. In fact, I was not even allowed to open the door of the apartment when somebody rang, as Arab thieves were likely visitors. But all the same I was prompt in answering every call. It was interesting, and of course I could always pretend to be fully obedient. Unluckily one day, when I was engaged in a lively conversation on the stairs, the door clicked shut. This door had an automatic lock, and I did not have the key. My mother found me on the door mat, and I was punished but not converted.

Another day I had my reward. An unknown and wonderful "uncle" appeared. I have referred to the half-brother of my mother who was once the youngest naval officer of France but was degraded for slapping his superior on the face and entered the *Légion étrangère*. The Foreign Legion is a very tough army corps famous for bravery and endurance. It is recruited from different nationalities. Often young men from good families who have committed some crime and escaped punishment choose to begin a new life there where nobody would ever ask about their past. They can even take another name but have to accept danger and strict discipline. They are sent wherever there is trouble. How interesting it was! I received my uncle very well after he explained who he was. I was generous in pouring out my father's best liquor for him. So he came back with two companions, men with bold gestures, tanned faces and a strange accent. I felt sure that they had as many stories as my grandfather. They had little time to tell them, however, as my father found them drinking his cognac to the health of his delighted daughter and smoking the expensive cigars that he kept for special friends. He was polite but firm. We did not see the heroes again. Perhaps none of them was really my uncle. My parents made inquiries about the identity of our visitors. This is the part of the story that I do not remember at all. Freud would probably infer that the conclusion was painful to me.

As I have no notes or any chronology of events, I cannot be sure of their order, but I believe that it was in these days that my mother introduced me to her place of work. This was a vast hall attached to the elegant Post Office of Casablanca, built in Moorish style with a columned façade and green tiles. In this hall, brilliantly lit day and night, there were many transmitting machines, some of them silently producing a small ribbon covered with dots or characters, but most of them noisily tapping, clicking or blinking signals that had to be decoded by a number of attentive employees. The boss, "*M. le Controleur*", was walking from one table to the other. The machines were quite interesting in their diversity, and those who were working them smiled at me; but only one thing fascinated me: the bald head of the "*controleur*", or supervisor. I believe that in those days most men kept their hair even in old age. Anyway, I had never seen a completely bald man, and the effect under the bright light was irresistible. I ran toward him, crying above the noise of the machines: "Mama, his top shines! How it shines!" The object of my admiration became surprisingly pinker, and my mother hurried out with me. For my part, I wondered, especially after a good scolding, what was wrong in pointing out something that looked rather a precious particularity to me. When father said that at seven it was time to be more "tame", I did not understand.

They both loved me after a fashion, though they longed for a calmer life. This first unfortunate attempt at parenthood discouraged them from trying again, and I remained an only child. They often yielded to me when I wanted something strongly enough. What I wanted then was to travel by plane. It was still a new way, quite uncomfortable and risky; but I was granted my wish: we would go to France by air! I had a few enjoyable nights dreaming of it. We took off in a small four-seater aircraft, very different in size, shape and convenience from the present-day jets. We were fastened to our seats and could never leave them. The small compartment was locked. We were constantly tossed and shaken, but it was wonderful to look down at the brown earth and white towns of Morocco. We were soon flying into the Spanish skies. The Rock between the two seas of slightly different hues was very majestic in the sunset. We could see little of Spain, where we had two stops and badly organized meals, and at dawn we gained some altitude before crossing the Pyrenees. We had been warned that there were some air pockets above this mountainous region, but we did not expect to fall, as to our death, into holes of one hundred, two hundred, three hundred meters and, after a shock following the dizzying fall, to climb again, only to fall anew, never knowing if, this time, it would not be to the ground. The plane protested with all its strained metal sheets, and we were bruised, still tied to our seats.

Mother was sick and was told that looking out the window made it worse; but she was curious to see the snowy mountains below. She compromised by looking at them with only one eye, shutting the other with her hand. It made me laugh, and I began to form the impression that in reality she was the child and I was the adult. My father was to confirm this not too modest opinion when, before his political tours of the country, he entrusted to me the care of the house even before I was ten. He even hinted about the kind of menus we should have for the few days he was away, and we never told him that we so often replaced meat by ice cream and vegetables by pickles. To come back to our plane, I enjoyed even the air pockets until father offered me a sandwich filled with the strongest wild boar meat he could have found as an unlikely meal for such a journey. Then I, too, began to long to be on the ground. France looked all vivid green after the rocks and snows of the Spanish side of the Pyrenees. We used to go to Europe for a three-month holiday every two or three years. I was glad to see Tante Jeanne and my grandparents again, and I will say more later on about these journeys. Lost as I am in the chronological sequence of events, I don't know if this air adventure preceded or followed the dreadful trip that I will now try to relate. Maybe the one by plane was during the Spanish war and the other just before.

To go to Europe we usually took one of the luxury boats from North Africa and spent three or four days sunning ourselves on the deck, swimming in the pool and laughing at leaping porpoises. I was never seasick and could never get enough of waves and wind. But sometimes we drove through Spain so we could use our car for the rest of our holidays in France, Italy or Switzerland. One spring when my parents were intending to cross through Spain, I developed oversized boils. I soon had eight of them and could not find any position where I could lie down without leaning on at least one of them with acute pain. Antibiotics had not yet been discovered, and the doctor was afraid of a general infection of the blood. But the worst was when, together with all the other boils that were very slow in maturing, I had one in each middle ear. Then I knew what physical suffering is and how, beyond a certain threshold, it can annihilate a person and even more so a child. There was nothing anywhere but throbbing pain. Sometimes I thought my head was aflame or that I would go mad. And to crown it all, I caught whooping cough. The violent, uncontrollable coughs shaking my whole body spread thousands of sparks from this fire everywhere in me. My ears were like cascades of pain. And we started our journey on the bad roads of Spain.

We slept in hotels, and my mother was annoyed because I could not keep down my food and soiled the carpets or blankets of the rooms, and she showed displeasure. This hurt, too, though she did not scold me. But more was to come. When we arrived at Brest I was taken to a doctor. Grandfather Le Théo had said that he was a good doctor. Only he was a "marine doctor," used to rough sailors and not to little girls. He said that he had to open the boils in my ears. No anesthesia. He sat down, caught my waist between his knees, had my head firmly held by a helper and pierced the boils as he intended, together with my eardrums as he had not intended. The infected fluid from the boils drained down my throat, choking me. When I became conscious again, my parents led me out and met some acquaintances near the door of the flat. They stopped briefly, and I suppose that they had to exchange a few words and smiles, but children know little about polite conventions. Though I felt incapable of any impression other than this dreadful physical pain, their smiles did reach me and pierced my heart as surely as the doctor's scalpel had just pierced my ears. Here I was, in such an intensity of pain, and my parents were smiling! I felt betrayed and utterly alone. It was an egotistic and childish reaction on my part, and I am certain that my parents were far from indifferent to my suffering. But for a moment I hated both of them for failing to reach out to me in compassion at the time of my greatest need.

I sank into a dark well of inexpressible solitude and stifling resentment that made the physical pain even more unbearable. I had never heard of those unfathomable depths of despair and isolation that Christians call "hell"; but, before

I was eight years old, in these circumstances, I may have had a certain taste of it. And it left forever in me a kind of sediment of loneliness, anguish and distrust. Never after that did I turn to any human being while in real distress, though I could share superficial disappointments with my friends. The nights and days that followed filled me with my first desire for death. Somehow my hearing was restored, though my eardrums kept their holes. I must have slowly recovered from the spreading infection, too; but I have no remembrance of the trip back to Casablanca three months later.

And what about the Lord during all this time? He was the One who saved me from despair. I knew he was, and I never ceased praying. With my cup filled with suffering, this prayer deepened.

Chapter VII

Like the Deer That Longs

The year after this cruel suffering, father bought a new car and decided to drive to Marrakech in order to break it in. This was not a clever choice, as we were supposed to go slowly for hundreds of kilometers until the different parts of the motor were worn in. Before reaching Marrakech, "the Queen of the Red Sands" at the foot of the Atlas Mountains, we had to cross, under a scorching sun, an immense plain, perfectly flat, which was an ocean of small stones. The road went from one side of the horizon to the other without so much as a bump or a small curve. In the total absence of trees, bush or grass, the only features above the ground were the poles of an electricity line, monotonously spaced along the perfectly straight road furrowing through the flat, sunlit, rocky desert. And we had to go at a speed under fifty kilometers an hour. This was to me a divine journey: in the front of the car my parents were chatting away the tediousness of this slow progress through the stony wilderness. Accidents were not rare, because drivers fell asleep at the wheel. Alone in the back, I was silent, but the Lord was keeping me good company. I felt his presence, I spoke to him, I drank from an invisible source.

It was around this time that I was given a child's book of legendary stories of animals. Each had a full-page illustration: the geese of the Capitol, which woke up a sleeping garrison as enemies approached, the dog of Alcibiades, with tender eyes and short tail, and there, in all its majesty, the deer of Saint Hubert with a cross between its forked horns. What attracted my attention was the short text under the picture: "As the deer longs for running streams, my soul is longing for you, my God" (Ps 42). This was my first tiny contact with Scripture. This was the only bit of the Bible I was to know for years. But it was immediately enshrined in my heart. It expressed perfectly my interior attitude, and I was to repeat it thousands of times. I believe that during this journey I was effortlessly in continuous prayer, and maybe I would have become a real friend of Christ in the midst of militant atheism if I had been faithful to this grace. It was all the more pure because I did not know anything about methods of prayer and "spiritual states", but I did know something instinctively about conscience as the voice of God, and too often I shut my heart to it or hardened it against inspirations of forgiveness and self-denial.

I loved Marrakech. A forest of graceful palm trees yielding a golden harvest of dates surrounded the red city in its crenellated ramparts. It was all built in *pisé*: laterite (red clay) mixed with chopped straw, which shines like mica in the thick walls of dried clay. Such were the buildings at which the Egyptians made their Hebrew slaves work. In the background, the Atlas mountains thrust into the blue sky, their summits always covered with sparkling snow. The town was very picturesque, and I was to know it better later on.

We had to return home for the reopening of school, and soon the light in me became dim, not in itself, for the faith was there, completely untouched, but obscured by much fog from an unsatisfactory moral life. I was strong-willed but following my own fancies. My father was still my teacher, my hero and my model, though I was aware in some ways of my feminine personality and never rejected it, even when fully hostile to my mother. But my father himself was eating from a full basket of contradictions. He was very intelligent and a passionate reader, but his education and readings were one-sided: general literature and Marxist sociology. Nor did he take any time to better his position, though some of his friends who did not have his ability successfully passed examinations giving access to higher or more lucrative jobs. All the time left by his professional duties was given to his party or his unions. My mother resented this. He had, however, a good salary as principal of the biggest school in the country, and his war years and Eastern Morocco service enabled him to receive more benefits; mother had her own salary, and I was an only child. As French people in a "protectorate", we were also in a rather colonial situation, though not colonialists. But it did not seem to father that he was in a "privileged class". He still looked on himself as one of the mythical "workers" who form the ideal socialist state. He never had doubts about his right to own a house with marble mosaic floors or to hire one and often two servants. It is true that he was kind to them, but sometimes I wondered why I was supposed to share my toys with their children when he never shared his car with their husbands. He was leader of the teachers' union of Morocco and also had something to do with the other unions, but he was married to a beautiful young woman who was greatly in need of his attention and support. He was a widely respected leader and a stern intellectual, and many of his "comrades" feared him, but children were his friends, and with them he showed an unsmiling but successful humor. One story became famous.

When a boy lost a milk tooth and, according to a European custom, expected a fairy to bring him some sweets for it, father went to the school museum and took one of the loose teeth of the stuffed crocodile that graced it. Somehow he made the child believe that this was the tooth he had lost—only it had grown! The child very happily and proudly paraded "his" tooth the whole afternoon. His mother was phoned and agreed laughingly to provide a proportionate bag of sweets. I am sure she returned the crocodile tooth, as my father was so scrupulous about government property.

I did not share this kind of scruple, but I appreciated my father's replacing everything he took from school. One day he broke some device accidentally, and in compensation he bought a series of art reproductions. Amidst profane works of art, I saw the Vladimir Icon, so well known in our days; and I am glad that this was my first religious picture. On another occasion, not hampered by my father's scrupulosity, I stole some mercury from the same museum. My aim was highly scientific. I had heard that mercury, as soon as it touches another metal, makes alloy with it. There were different metals in my mother's jewel box, enough for a scientific experiment! The box was of Arabic design, very cleverly made of many bits of wood. You had to move them in a particular sequence to open it. I had already broken the code, and I took hold of all the jewels in order to make the experiment more credible. It was wonderful. As soon as a silver chain, a gold ring or bracelet touched a drop of mercury, lo! it became mercury, like oiled silver. I did not know that it was far more difficult to make them return to their original state through heating the metal without melting it or letting the stones fall out. The reaction of the family can be imagined. But nothing could discourage my scientific investigations. Only I was not lucky. One day I deftly stole the egg bags of some big spiders and treasured them in my cupboard under my best linen. Why did mother have to check my handkerchiefs just after all those creatures hatched?

I had a worse case when we were told that everything kept humid and warm produced different kinds of mold and tiny mushrooms, but the species had to be kept separated. There was a particular dresser in the dining room that was rarely opened. It sheltered from clumsy hands a delicate china dinner-set used only for special guests. Soon pieces of meat were nicely rotting in the soup plates and a month-dead fish occupied the salad dish; old pieces of bread carefully kept humid with chicken soup, wine and other beverages were particularly successful. How attractive all these green hues and how graceful the minute forests of tender stems ending in white balls! The problem was that no amount of scrubbing and washing could take off the yellow stains left on china by this new kind of garden. I was at school when "special" visitors came to our house, and I had a sad homecoming that day. I could fill this copybook with stories of this kind alone, but enough of it.

The reason why I was most often scolded, however (and it was extremely tiresome), was that I did not want to eat. I never felt hungry until I began swimming, and I was secretly stuffing my pockets with everything our dog or cat could eat from my plate. It is regrettable that our Alsatian puppy got not only my meat but all the calcium that the doctor ordered for me during my young years. The dog ended with magnificent teeth, and I with weak vertebrae. I liked only *couscous*, chocolates and coconut cookies. One day my mother baked a full plate of them and warned me: "They are counted!" I did not know that she was preparing for a party. When the day came she found out, unfortunately in front of the guests, that, although the number had not changed, a tiny part of each cake was missing, and many bore the mark of small front teeth. Even in trivial happenings like this our lack of mutual trust showed. I certainly deserved to be scolded, maybe punished, but not humiliated in front of our friends with the hint that I had acted out of malice and spite rather than out of childish greediness. On my side, I resented her handling of the situation as one of the signs that she did not love me.

My father was more controlled, though he was also angered on two occasions. Once we went to a birthday dinner at the house of some affluent people, not really our friends. With the help of another child, I took some precious little curios from the drawing room and transferred them into the deep pocket of my father's coat. This coat was not often used. It was only several days later that its load was discovered, and it was with much embarrassment (he had no training in humility) that my father had to return the curios to their surprised owner.

Something more tragic happened during one of our journeys through Spain. That year we stopped at Granada, and the Moorish grace, the rich decoration of the Alhambra, seemed to us between dream and reality. We also visited the Seville cathedral, where ladies in mantillas fan themselves during the sermons with large, ornate fans. I admired their clever way of opening and shutting their fans with an almost imperceptible movement of the wrist. At Madrid, all the Velasquez of the Prado museum looked down disapprovingly at me. We went to a rather luxurious hotel because the exchange rate was very favorable to French travelers. As we wanted to be early on the road to San Sebastian, my father paid the bill the evening before. While his attention and the cashier's were elsewhere for an instant, I withdrew the large note that father had just put on the desk and slipped it into my pocket. It was only to use my old skill and an almost reflex act, given the favorable circumstances that my friend Thomas had taught me to recognize. I had no interest in the money itself. But there was a loud confrontation as my father claimed his change and the cashier demanded his due. Nobody thought of the innocent-looking little girl beside the desk. When we were in our rooms, I saw that my father was very upset and I went to him: "Papa, is it because of this note that you are so annoyed? Here it is. You may return it." And I pulled it out of my pocket. He had never been so cross with me. What made it worse was that obviously the hotel staff thought that he had taught me the trick and was just frightened into returning the note. I, too, was annoyed. After all, what was wrong in taking some money from these capitalists? We could even have given it to some proletarian worker, thus reestablishing a bit of justice in the world. We left Madrid before dawn in full disagreement with one another. Mother could not even speak to me. I am afraid that up to now, notwithstanding the fact that I have never stolen anything knowingly since my first Communion, I have still never understood much about private property. The injustice of the actual distribution of riches has always been far more obvious to me than the right to privilege. Some of the socially accepted forms of hypocrisy repelled me, too. I would have died rather than pretend to love someone I did not love, though for my mother it was just "politeness".

The three of us were making a mess of our family life, though, likely enough, little would have been needed to mend our relationship. For me it would have been far better to have had brothers and sisters. Father should never have married my mother. During my childhood she always seemed wrong to me and my father right. Later on I understood that this judgment was unfair. He loved her but neglected her, and she could not bear to be neglected. She needed attention, time and a cheerful environment. She loved dresses, novels and society; but she was not superficial and could sacrifice herself, too. However, she did not show any desire to participate in what her husband was doing in his useful public life or to share the search, sufferings and joys of her daughter in a personal manner.

As a self-centered and inexperienced child, I could not see that we were all responsible for the disharmony of our relationship. Father was rarely home. Often he had political meetings up to two or three o'clock in the morning. Mother was anxious and lonely; but when he returned home, he was tired and still full of ideas and arguments. Then he paid hardly any attention to the beautiful but frustrated young woman at his side. And she did not want to hear of his struggle for peace or justice. She had plenty of admirers who sent her flowers and notes. Without encouraging this homage, she did enjoy her feminine successes. She even spoke of them to me, and this revolted me. She was innocent enough in her little vanities and had no joy at home between her passionately involved, intellectual husband and a secretive, intense, sometimes hostile child whom she did not understand and whom she left in loneliness even when she tried to please her. One day she wanted a new dress and renounced it to offer me the kind of fashion she liked for herself. I refused it because it did not suit me. I wanted to wear simple sports clothing, not lace and ribbons. She was hurt. So was I when she misinterpreted my reactions, and so was my father when she dismissed his labors as useless.

When I was with mother in town, many men casually remarked on her beauty. It irked me that she was pleased with their admiration. She was intelligent but not interested in philosophical questions, not even in literature, while my father and I could recite by heart thousands of verses from classical plays or modern poetry and discuss ideas when I was barely ten. In fact, my father made me read Renan and Voltaire before that age, and he could make me understand a difficult text just by the way he read it. Mother did not share this interest but enjoyed discussing pictures. It is rather surprising that she preferred meaningful film scenarios, while my father delighted in westerns and detective stories. I suppose that they rested his mind. I did not follow his tastes. We were living in constant, open or unexpressed conflict, and I suffered most intensely, because I was still fragile and incomplete and because my parents also had a professional world in which they had good relationships and interests that I did not have. I hated school. At times the tensions were quite unbearable for all of us, and this in spite of the fact that there was also a kind of frustrated love in our hearts. The Spirit often inspired me to yield and to forgive. Though I did try to do so at times, I am afraid that too often I protected myself from the insistent demands upon me.

The environment did not help. I was even dragged to political meetings at night in an atmosphere of smoke and cheap drink. Often the meetings were held in the basement of a big café. The Communists were leading, and little by little the call for hatred and violence was finding an echo in me. Jesus says that "the meek will possess the land." This is no more obvious than "happy are those who mourn." Having been involved for so long with the Communist Party, I believe that much of its past success came from the fact that it makes a constant appeal to our aggressive instincts, while Christianity is far more occupied in controlling, taming and reducing them. To link what is best in man: love of justice, compassion and desire for a harmonious society with all the strength of hatred, revolt, readiness for battle and triumph over one's enemies is a tremendous asset. Hating injustice and oppression is perfectly natural, and all children have a deep sense of fairness. Developing this into hatred of the unjust and oppressors is very easy. Then you have only to point out which "oppressors" have to be destroyed—by any means. When you allow yourself to hate, your heart hardens and becomes indifferent to other values. This was another disturbing element in my life, and I did not know how to integrate it when something in me, especially during my periods of prayer, was still speaking of universal love.

Chapter VIII

The Villa

Unsatisfied with their apartment, my parents decided to build their own house with a loan from an association of war veterans. For almost one year, every weekend my father took me to the site of our building, not far from the lycée where I would have my secondary education. I believe I was about seven when these visits began, and I enjoyed them greatly. My father looked relaxed, and we were good companions. It was interesting to watch the work progressing: the basement with its cellars, laundry and garage, the beautiful mosaic floor, where thousands of small pieces of colored marble were inserted in intricate designs, the drawing room and dining room with the veranda taking shape, then my parents' bedroom and my own, a large room with two windows looking out onto different parts of the garden, a big hall that was to hold a Ping-Pong table, and the kitchen with its little court. There were fair-sized flower beds all around the house and a pretty roof in ceramic tiles. As the building rose, my union with my father reached new depths. He would tell me about his ideas and readings or about his ambitions, which were all altruistic: to better the life of the teachers, both Moslem and French, and their influence in the country, especially in fighting "the forces of obscurantism that continually stream from the Catholic Church", and in opposing the rise of a new, semi-Fascist party, "the Cross of Fire", his enemies. I responded well enough but could never speak of my own inner life, of my struggles, of my fears. This year, however, I was less lonely.

My cousin was not with us, as his parents could not immediately obtain a transfer to the capital. They were at Beni-Mellal, a village in the Atlas Mountains. I was sent there for two Christmas holidays and was immersed in paradisal beauty. The village of small ochre and white dwellings rested in a grove of rugged, silvery olive trees. The rich dark earth's fertility had been preserved and increased by centuries of skillful farming and was watered with pure springs from the mountains' snows. No castle in Europe could have the garden that surrounded my aunt's modest house. Thousands of roses bloomed in a splendid variety of color, size and shape on graceful branches above our heads and all around us. Giant violets grew under the fruit trees. Near the village, line after line of well-tended orange trees produced delicious fruit, as big as a child's head. These were the navel variety and perfect in shape and color. We were often offered dark-leaved branches heavy with bright orange fruit. Olives were crushed under enormous round stones, and the golden oil was stored in elegant clay jars near the golden wheat. The people were simple, happy and more friendly than in other parts of the country. The birds and insects were singing in sound or color. Eagles and storks met in the pure, luminous air. I was soon to love Virgil because his bucolics reminded me of Beni-Mellal. But there were scorpions in this paradise, and my aunt slept in terror of letting a corner of her sheet fall down and be an easy ladder for these poisonous creatures. The legs of our beds were always dipped in tins filled with petrol. Sometimes, however, I took deadly scorpions in my hand without being harmed.

Often, beautiful young girls, their hands and cheeks decorated with henna and their long braids woven with silver coins and ribbons, came to offer us rich silk embroideries. They looked quite free, as they were Shluhs, not Arabs. The French Administration provided them with schools and dispensaries but respected the way of life of these wise people. It was a feast for me to visit them.

We entered our new home a little before my eighth birthday. I liked it but was very shocked to find that around all the switches and door handles my father had ordered chromium sheets to be fixed. They were very shiny and, in my judgment, still unchanged, very ugly. To my indignant inquiries, he answered that these expensive metal protections were to keep the walls free of stains, even if our maids were not careful in cleaning their hands. I was to be most often alone in this villa, my father being busy elsewhere and my mother having strange hours of work. So it happened that the very day after we took possession of it, I was on my own the whole afternoon, meditating resentfully on the chromium plaques. Then I had an idea. I went to the still-empty garden and took a handful of rough sand and small stones. Then I energetically rubbed each one of the "protective sheets". The result was a great disorder of crisscrossed lines, but at least they were not shiny anymore. Though exhausted, I was quite happy, until my parents returned. So did I keep my reputation of being a "difficult child" even when I was filled with good intentions. Glass replaced chromium, and it was certainly less aesthetically offensive.

My mother would work one day from 8:00 A.M. to 1:30 P.M. and then from 7:00 P.M. to 9:00 P.M., and the following day from noon to 7:30 P.M. It took her half an hour to go to and from the Post Office, as father needed the car. This made normal family life impossible, as my father and I were keeping school hours. The extreme irregularity of our meals must have been part of my difficulties in taking food. When my mother ended her day at 8:00 P.M., father had to fetch her for security reasons. We never had more than one meal a day together and often none at all. When we did have it, my father was often listening to the news or answering the phone, and my mother cooking and eating at the same time. The maids rarely slept in the house.

On Thursdays there were no classes; neither, of course, on Sundays. Then I was alone all the time. I could not even have the company of classmates. When I began secondary school, I was only nine and found again the problem of being with much older girls. Besides, many of them were Catholic, and my father would not have them in our house. So I had no friends. I sometimes escaped on my bicycle and went to explore the other parts of the town where only Moslems (the Medina) or Jews (the Mellah) lived. But most of the time I remained home, reading and reading and reading everything that came under my eyes. When I heard a key in the lock, I threw the book on top of a cupboard and pretended to be busy at my homework; but I hardly did any homework at all. As I was also encouraging a lack of discipline, I was in trouble with my teachers, and school was a very unpleasant place for me. I always had the first place effortlessly in literature and in some other subjects if they captured my attention or if I liked the teacher, but I got bad marks in everything that required a bit of virtuous application. Anyway, what was the use of it? Sometimes I reflected that, if somebody had ever asked me to act for God's love, I would have done anything required of me. But it never happened, and I had not learned to recognize God's will in duty. I developed a skill in inventing and telling stories, and for a few months I had companions listening spellbound to them during recreations. But the supervisors intervened because they wanted the children to play. So I returned to books: novels, history, politics, poetry. There was no Christian book at home, and I could not draw any either from the municipal library, but in general literature I came across some religious texts and they overwhelmed me. A page of Pascal or a medieval *fabliau* could provoke such strong emotions in me that it left me crying. I did not know that God could also touch our hearts of flesh, and I took this phenomenon to be a kind of illness. Through all these hours of reading, many during the night, my eyes were dimming but my mind expanding.

One of my discoveries could have been dangerous. Father had a private cupboard with a lock that I could not manage. I had no peace until I found a key to open it. There were confidential papers about the vices of some teachers: some were drinking, one had an immoral life, another was going to Mass every day and the last one was dangerously violent. I also found the love letters of my parents—very poetic! I visited the cupboard from time to time, and one day (I must have been twelve, as I remember that I was falling in love with Greek) I discovered a few books of pornography. Both my parents were decent, sound people, so these books must have been confiscated by my father at school and thrown there instead of more wisely burned. The books repelled, amazed and shocked me, but I read them all. Something far more dangerous for me was an initiation to drugs. This was very attractive. There was always ether in our medical supplies, and I liked the smell of it. What about getting drunk? Then something entered my heart. From the Lord I had never received moral instruction, only bits of catechism. But this time I "knew" that I had to renounce forever the forbidden cupboard and the delights of experiencing ether or other drugs, or I would never hear again the silent voice of my Master. I was strangely torn. After a struggle, without enthusiasm but driven by something more powerful than me, I shut the cupboard, climbed the wall at the back of our garden and threw the key far away into a still unbuilt plot covered with grass and wild bushes.

Some days later I had a strange experience, the only one like it in my life. It was a peaceful, warm evening, and before going to bed I opened my window to breathe some fresh air. The stars were very bright, as usual at that time of the year. But suddenly they appeared to be growing, moving and meeting, forming a silvery background of light against which a shape like an immense, black bird of prey was outlined. In a moment the creature was on me. I was terrified and completely unable to move. The monster took me by the shoulders, where he dug his sharp claws. I was beginning to be lifted up when I cried voicelessly to God. Then I felt rooted to the floor by an enormous weight. Soon I found myself alone, shaken in soul and body. My shoulders remained painful for several days. Long years later I wondered if this had been a psychosomatic reaction, an unconscious interpretation of my moral struggle about the cupboard or my own "shadow". I do not think it possible. At the time I felt sure that I had had an encounter with evil in a personal form. I had never paid any attention to the medieval stories I read about the devil; and I was a reckless child, unafraid of even real danger. But then I knew what fear was. I was often alone in the house even during the night and remembered the creature "prowling in the dark, searching for a prey to devour". I never said anything about this or any other fear, and silence did not help me to grow out of it. I did not even pray about it. Something dark had come over me again, and I wanted to forget it.

I was not completely alone, though, because I loved animals and they usually loved me, too. I had two exceptional pets, both very big for their kind, intelligent and handsome: an Alsatian shepherd and a giant Siamese cat. She certainly preserved herself from my tyranny better than the dog did. I could say as much as Colette, the French writer, though not with her talent, about my cat. Even if it makes it too long, I don't see how I could write my own tale without some animal stories. True Siamese cats are particularly wild and intelligent, and Mitsou was an exceptionally gifted Siamese. From the time I came back from Brittany, she had been my ever-ready playmate. My hands and arms were always covered with scratches, but I did not mind, and I never complained about her nor she about me, though we had our private disputes. She understood me perfectly. One day a visitor came for dinner with a new hat, a stupid thing like those inverted flower pots that some English ladies cherish. In fact it even had satin flowers. My aesthetic sense was again offended, but I knew what would happen if I threw the hideous thing into the fire. Instead I explained everything to Mitsou and shut her in with the hat. Half an hour later there was not a bit of hat bigger than a nail left of this new purchase. I kept my friend hidden for a while and brought her a nice fish from the fridge as a reward. Anyway, even mother said that the hat was ridiculous.

Sometimes Mitsou acted on her own. She was very jealous and possessive. In the drawing room we had a large Arabic vase with original designs, on a Moroccan stand inlaid with mother-of-pearl. Most people who visited us went to admire this valuable piece of local art and paid attention to the giant Siamese only afterward. One day we found the vase broken in pieces on the carpet and the cat waiting for attention and praise of her beauty in the exact place that the vase had occupied on the stand. The only time we could have stopped being friends was when I undertook to dust her with the vacuum cleaner. It sucked her hair powerfully, and she became completely wild, jumping and clawing here and there and finally tearing at all the curtains. I was so afraid of her going mad that I called mother, but there was nothing we could do except let the cat calm down. The cat and I were both punished.

We shared many more adventures together, and she always slept in my room. One evening when I went on an errand, I found her dead in the street, knocked down by a car. My sorrow and sense of bewilderment were so deep that I could not sleep, work or eat normally for days. The dead body of this magnificent cat in my arms seemed to be the weight of all the fragility, the unreliability of life. My parents said reproachfully that I was mourning more for the cat than for my grandmother. She had died a few months before, on November first. She had told grandfather, "We shall visit the cemetery today. Please cut your best chrysanthemums." He went down to the garden and, when he came back, found her dead from a heart attack. The chrysanthemums that she had asked for were laid on her own coffin. I had been sad, but grandmother had been living far away in France, and Mitsou had always been with me, sharing my play, my loneliness and my fears. Grandfather was with us at the time, and he thought to console me by secretly skinning the cat. Having prepared the large, beautiful skin with much care, he put it triumphantly on my bed. How I cried anew! I could hardly forgive him for substituting a sign of more complete death for a living presence. Again everyone was puzzled at my reaction. If they did not want me to get attached to animals, why did they not give me a brother or sister or spend more time with me? Those were my thoughts, but I said nothing.

The dog was not so much my companion, because he was not admitted inside the house. But he, too, was a splendid animal, grown strong and tall on raw meat, rice and my own remedies. I trained him very carefully. He did not obey anybody else, but he obeyed me perfectly and was tolerant of my parents. I could leave a piece of meat between his paws with an order to refrain from touching it and then go to school. Coming back I always found the poor animal still in Tantalus' torment, looking with wet mouth and crossed eyes at the untouched meat. I trained him to take a quick run in the street at anybody I pointed out to him, looking intent on devouring him (or usually her) on the spot; then, when he was just upon the victim with flashing fangs, I would stop him almost in midair. This interesting exercise did not endear me to the ladies of our neighborhood, and when one of them, a veiled Moslem woman who could look at the dog only through a hole in her muslin mask, almost fainted, I generously gave up the fun. He was a good guardian but once mistook a friend for a foe and left him with a missing calf. I was very sorry.

One of the best things that could ever have happened to me when I was eight was that the town where I grew up was endowed with a very large swimming pool. If it had been an ordinary one, smallish and even perhaps surrounded by buildings, I would not have cared for such a place. On the other hand, my parents would not have let me swim alone in the ocean, which was quite dangerous there with its treacherous currents, high waves, reefs, whirlpools and electric fish. It was this that made the government spend so much money on a pool. It was the second in the world for size (after one in Los Angeles, I believe) and built like a natural part of the shore. It was completely surrounded by rocks or sea, according to the tide. In fact, at high tides the waves continually crashed on the low bottom walls and invaded the pool with salty showers and light white spray. I was to be proud of belonging to the foolish gang of youngsters who sat down on these walls for the thrill of being projected into the middle of the pool at the next attack of the ocean and at the risk of broken bones or drowning. This, of course, was only one of the forbidden pleasures to be discovered.

Besides a very large pool where hundreds of persons could bathe or swim together, there was a shallower one for children and a secluded one for the training of good swimmers, with white lines on blue floors and an Olympic diving board twenty meters high. In this last pool I was to spend at least two hours a day for close to six years. The training pool was surrounded by a vast amphitheater, where large crowds of spectators could come and watch the competitions, but on Sundays only. I preferred the place private and silent, when I could be alone in the water, at one with the ocean, surrounded only by the music of its waves and the cry of its gulls, or sometimes with a few companions of the same mind, obliging the body to be as familiar with the sea as with the air. Soon I would also be teaching children to swim. Far from merely transmitting a skill, I felt as if I were initiating them into some sacred mystery or a higher life. Only a few responded to this view. My family was happy when I won a race, especially if it was a public occasion. I do not think it ever counted with me. In fact, crowds were a great hindrance when I specialized in high-diving. But this was not before I was almost fourteen.

Meanwhile, I liked even the monotonous hours of training, when I had to repeat the same movement for hours on end under the stern rule of the coach. "Your right shoulder should be lower when you turn. Your toes are not extended. Your left elbow should be raised. Try again. And again. And again. Today the task is two kilometers without ever using your arms." And there I was, my hands still on a small board and my feet making foam with the fast regular beat that alone propelled me. Two kilometers in sea water is a long distance, and others protested, but I was content. I knew that I would conquer the ocean in my small persevering way after all this was performed. I was ready also for the harsh discipline: to renounce pictures, parties or even reading for lack of time, to keep my weight down, to swim all winter in icy water, to elongate my muscles by slow, careful exercise. I was not so good at speed swimming because my lungs were small, but I could maintain a good rhythm on long distances. Often, however, I was so tired that I was hardly able to jump on my bicycle and go home along the beautiful, palm-tree-lined avenue. There and in the solitude of the pool (even when we were several swimmers together, we trained silently) I often met with my Lord in confident gratitude and deep longing "like the deer for running streams".

Home was not really home, but we often had interesting visitors. I must have been ten or twelve when we had German friends with us for some days. On a weekend we all went to a beach. They were all extremely fair, the young man and his wife and their two children, all with transparent skin in great need of a tan, yellow hair and clear blue eyes. I was almost jealous because the man was so uninhibitedly tender with his children. My father said that I should play with them, but he did not speak about these visitors as he was wont to do about others. I asked why, and he said rather casually: "Because they are anarchists. This man has put a bomb under a train, and eight people were killed. The German police are after him." I asked, "But if he killed people, why do you hide him?" "Oh," said father, "the victims were Fascist people." And he stopped me talking. I was very puzzled.

My father was such a pacifist, and this man here on this beach was such a lamb.

I was to experience this puzzlement again, but in a variant expression when I met the "Pasionaria", Dolores Sbaruri. She was the leader of the Spanish Communist Party during the civil war. She died in Spain, in 1989, after spending the Franco years in Russia. Horrid stories circulated about her, especially that she had killed priests by cutting their jugular vein with her own teeth. The fact is that she sent many of them to their death by firing squad and some to torture. So I was disappointed to see this dark, small, quite ordinary-looking woman in front of us on a stage. I think that father was near her on the red-veiled tribune. Mother and I were in the front among the left-wing militants, and behind there must have been more than ten thousand people ready to applaud or whistle. We were all talking and moving chairs when suddenly she spoke. The silence was instantaneous and total. The feminine and slightly raucous voice soared and dominated everything. I did not notice whether there were loudspeakers or if she was speaking in Spanish or French. Somehow everybody heard, everybody understood, everybody vibrated. "We have to fight, fight to their death or ours. It is liberty that is at stake. It is justice. It is the very life of our people and your life, too, comrades of the whole world." This was the message, simple enough, but it came across with unbelievable natural power. She was a tempest, a volcano. She was burning and whipping and arousing in you all the revolts you did not know were there. After the storm she was again an ordinary little Spanish woman worker. But whoever you were, you were not the same after listening to her cry.

We had Moslem friends, too, some of modest condition, a bus conductor whose children had been in my father's class and a Koranic teacher who had two wives. These two women lived in peace and harmony, helping one another with the household duties and the care of their several beautiful children. Their faces were unveiled when they greeted my father, but they withdrew immediately, letting a male servant provide us with boiling minted tea and honeyed biscuits. With my mother, they were gay and curious, but she did not speak Arabic and they knew little French. They were all deeply religious people, and I wondered why my father could not bear any allusion to God but had no problem with Allah.

We were acquainted with some very rich people, too, though I do not know how. One *Kaid* (Arab nobleman) had an extremely refined dwelling. Outside there was not much difference between his house and the adjoining ones; all were whitewashed, with heavy wooden doors decorated with copper knobs and knockers. We were usually admitted by a man in a white *gandourah* (an ample alb-like garment) and red *chechia* (cap); and beyond a shadowy porch we found ourselves in a princely patio where slender mosaic columns emulated the graceful palm trees in the central garden. In the sparkling marble basins, fresh fountains were always rising and falling, sculpted plaster lace graced the vaults, and from there the perfume of jasmine and roses filled the rooms, which all opened on the veranda's enclosed garden. Servants brought us orange blossoms in fresh water and pies of dove wings. Sometimes there were twenty chickens to one meal, each one prepared in a different way, and a multitude of cakes and sweetmeats. Mama, who enjoyed these receptions, was called into the harem of some twenty wives and concubines, and you could hear exclamations of wonder at the extraordinary and rather scanty way the European women dressed when her clothing was minutely examined.

I liked to sit on the low sofas covered with rich blankets or brocade and loaded with cushions of delicately embroidered satin, taking in all the beauty around us, the silver firearms and golden curved knives in their engraved shields on the walls, between precious hangings of tapestry or embossed leather (but no pictures), the deep carpets of dyed wool and the low furniture intricately carved and inlaid, the ceramic bowls filled with fragrant blossoms. Our hosts were extremely polite and subtly contemptuous. There was certainly no blind admiration for the colonialist *Rumis* in the heart of the Moroccans, even of the lower classes.

I also knew something of the North African underworld through meeting with strange personalities in the Communist or Socialist Parties and visiting crowded slums. One of them was horrifying in its squalor and its monsters, people without arms and legs or with too many of them and fingers in the most unlikely places, even one boy with two heads. They had to pay rent for the small place where they tried to build a cardboard and tin shelter, and father was up in arms to denounce the shameful exploiters who were getting rich on the misery of twenty thousand families. There were also many lame or blind men (where were the women?— probably killed) in the narrow streets, but the Moslems were faithful to their law of almsgiving, at least for the feasts.

Things were getting worse at home. For weeks my parents had been arguing in the evening, though stopping when I was around. One day mother came to me and said: "Mr. X. [a very rich man, in his early thirties, kind and free] wants to marry me. Should I go with him or remain with you?" I answered: "I am not the one to decide." I have regretted this answer ever since. I did not mean to be cruel, but I thought it best that she go. Father would not renounce his work, and she would not even try to share his interests.

She never showed either that she wanted to understand me as being different from herself, and so I could not have a normal relationship with her. She left at once. When father came I told him. He took the car. Two hours later he was back with mother, who was silent and subdued, and his suit was in disorder. When we were alone I asked what happened. He answered between clenched teeth, "I gave him a beating, and I brought her home." We never again spoke of it. I could not even apologize to my mother but tried to show kindness to her afterward.

Meanwhile, I had some opportunities to learn the wisdom of obedience. One day especially, having a bad sore throat, which often happened, I left my bed in spite of a very high fever but was accidentally seen by my uncle and thereafter watched for several days. I succeeded in escaping anyway and again climbed the outer wall of the garden, walking on the narrow top until I became very dizzy and could see myself falling to my death. It was with very great difficulty that I jumped and came back to my room.

It was not better at school. I was most annoying, and my teachers had had enough of the disorder I created. We finally reached a climax. I had organized a concourse of noises during the geography class, which I found boring—a soft whistle here, a grunt there, a cock-a-doodle-doo in a corner. It was quite successful. My first accomplice and I were kept in after class to copy Latin verbs (yes, it was still done) in a locked classroom. We had an argument. It was winter. I covered my hands with soot from the stove and rubbed them energetically on the face of my unwilling companion. After she cried, it was even better. A most original carnival figure! This time there was a "disciplinary council" for me, and most of my teachers wanted me dismissed. Then the principal of the school, who had never seemed to know me, stood up and said: "We should keep the child. She will soon change. There is no real evil in her, but she should be with girls closer to her age. Let her repeat her present class, though she has the marks to pass, and let none of us show her any distrust." The wise woman had her way. I was moved and did not want to disappoint her. Within a day my childish behavior disappeared.

Chapter IX

Friends

The following year I found my first friend, Claudine. She was to be almost the center of my life for more than two years. She was very bright and had Spanish features with a tanned face and deer-like eyes. We both shared a passion for swimming and lots of literary interests, and she was a Catholic, which meant that, even if I was received in her house, she was not allowed by my father to enter ours. I never told her anything about my own inner life but tried to get information from her. She gave me the weekly bulletins of the JEC (Catholic students association) and certainly prayed much for my conversion, though her attitude was very discreet.

I had just read the Gospel of Saint John in the language in which it was first written. It was given me as my first long reading in Greek, because John wrote it with a vocabulary of only five hundred words or so. I was caught up in its spiritual beauty and wanted to understand its full meaning. Youth is ambitious. The preceding year, in France at Vittel, I had skillfully opened the door of our neighbor, when I was sure she was out of the hotel. I had seen this old lady going to Mass, and, finding her missal on her night table, I stole it. But it did me little good, for I did not understand a thing, except one very precious prayer, the Our Father. I returned the missal as a useless piece of Christian literature, though I was to appreciate it highly in days to come, but I kept the Our Father in my heart for frequent use.

Now that my exterior life was less foolish, my interior life began to progress a little. I found the way back to some self-denial and to almost continuous prayer. When I was at school, I was often filled with a feeling of intense wonder, because there and everywhere I could reach God himself, address him as Father and be listened to, because there was a bridge so easy to cross between my utter smallness and the infinite greatness of his love.

I was also busy at the pool, where high-diving had taken hold of me. Mother was frantic because the last holder of the championship, a beautiful girl who had just celebrated her twentieth birthday, was lying forever on a bed, her spine broken. But nothing could deter me. When the chairwoman of a swimming club told my parents that this sport was very dangerous at my age, mother answered bitterly, "Do you know her? What do you expect us to do, tie her day and night to the foot of her bed?" I knew it was dangerous, and that was part of the fun. When you fall from a height of twenty meters with the speed of acceleration and the added density of salt water, you should enter the water at a given angle or risk breaking your bones. In the beginning, I hurt myself several times because one of my fingers was not straight or my ankles were a little bent. I did not like somersaults or other complicated figures as much as the perfection of one accomplished "Angel Dive". To climb swiftly to the fourth story of the "Olympic" diving board, to look around at the sky and at the ocean, which are both yours at that moment, to spring even higher than the highest board and to be flying with outstretched arms like a free bird, parallel to the water, before beginning the graceful curve downward and ordering all your muscles for the right harmonious balance, as well as the last shock and the entry into the water, perfectly straight from the tip of your fingers to your joined toes! Then to go deep and surface again with a powerful stroke upward. This was happiness! On the days of competitions, there were more risks. Once, when the amphitheater was filled with people, I had to perform a particularly dangerous dive. The organizer of the games asked for total silence, but before I reached the water the crowd began to applaud. I could feel the vibration all around me and almost lost my balance. But I dived alone often, and I never felt a touch of fear.

We had very good friends, the Tanguys, at Mogador. This is a city farther down on the Atlantic coast, and a very pretty one. It is quite windy there and the seas are rough; but the sands are safe and the reefs can be managed by a good swimmer. The city is enclosed in beautiful ramparts and Portuguese fortifications, and its streets are alive with manifold activities. Each one has its own corporation and street. Here many jewelers fashion gold and silver into tiny leaves and flowers on earrings, necklaces and rings. There you may hear the copper beaten where large round trays are decorated with the ubiquitous "rose of the sands". Farther on, leather is richly embroidered in bags, saddles and *babouches*, or precious pieces of furniture are carved and inlaid with different kinds of scented woods or mother-of-pearl. A riot of color is waiting for you in the market of dyed silks and cottons, hanging everywhere above your head and around you. When we did not go abroad for holidays, I was sent there for two or three months. It was good for me to share the life of a larger family, for our friends had four children. I marvelled at their appetite and at the freedom they knew how to mix with well-accepted discipline.

Part of the town was Jewish. Sabbath days saw the streets filled with yellow, purple and green silky dresses and men's black suits. The smell of heavy pastries came from many windows. A Jewish girl had suddenly disappeared from our school when she was thirteen. We heard that she had been sent to Mogador to marry an old rich man. I met her and she invited me to her new home, new for her but centuries old. The high-ceilinged rooms were dim, as heavy curtains obscured all the tall windows. A kind of phantom emerged from the wall when I entered the drawing room, but it was my own reflection in a highly polished silver mirror, the kind the crusaders brought to Europe in the thirteenth century. You could never be aware of somebody approaching, so deep were the carpets and so silent the heavy doors. The atmosphere of mystery and half-living past history was over-powering, and I was glad to be back in the din of the street and the glaring Moroccan sun.

Most of our time was spent near or in the ocean. I swam for hours in the cool water, and it was most often pleasant. But one day, when I was perhaps two miles from the shore, the wind rose with violence, and when I wanted to return I found myself facing waves that did not even allow for breathing. I was exhausted in no time and knew that I could never reach the beach. So I immersed myself as completely as possible in the water and let myself be tossed by the waves, waiting in the arms of my "mother" to be missed or searched for. The ocean then was more than ever the symbol of God to me. Someone looking at it with binoculars discovered me and sent a boat to rescue me after two or three hours. That day I found land quite all right! But I never learned to distrust the ocean. At the end of the same month I had a closer escape. Swimming far out again, I saw wonderful creatures, pink, blue and mauve, floating and moving on the water like large half-globes in colored glass touched by the sun. Soon they were upon me, and some of them fixed themselves on my arms, chest and legs. Hundreds of tiny tentacles injected their burning venom into my body. I tried to tear away the medusae from me, but I could only throw away handfuls of jelly-like flesh while all the tentacles still adhered to my body and many more attacked me. It was a horrible experience. I finally swam out of reach of the shoal of medusae, but I was quite sick afterward.

A few days later, on a calm evening, I went out alone to explore the Portuguese fortifications, their thick walls and rusty cannons. Climbing high on a rampart, I discovered a small room at the top of a worn-out flight of stairs. It was not locked. I pushed the door and found myself in a sacred place, a small chapel with windows on the ocean, shells on the altar and a flickering oil lamp before a crucifix and a veiled box. And there I found my Lord. I did not know how he was there and did not give form to the Presence, but I was immersed in it. A peaceful stillness came upon me while I looked in silent and thought-suspended awe at the tabernacle that was so mysteriously holding him. I often came back to the hidden cenacle, always empty but for the One who was living there between sky and sea. And it looked as if he was waiting for me. A great desire was soon burning in my heart. I obscurely sensed that Jesus was there as Food as well as Presence, and my heart sang even more often, "Like the deer for running streams, my soul is longing for you, my God."

I also had an intense time of adoration in the evening, during my last swim at sunset, when every drop of water was a sun and I was like one drowned in limitless beauty and glory.

The last year of my Mogador holidays, I noticed an old beggar who was often sitting on a small heap of stones against the wall of the main mosque. He was almost always alone and still, his eyes shut, though his head was erect. His emaciation as well as the holes in his greyish cape spoke of destitution so clearly that I decided to spare some coins for him. When I had a handful of them, I went to him and dropped them on his lap. He did not look up, and some of the coins rolled down into the dust. I retrieved them and opened his clasped hands to put the money in his wrinkled palms. I saw then that he was holding and slowly moving a long string of red beads, the Moslem rosary of ninety-nine praises of God (the hundredth one will be revealed in heaven): the All-merciful, the All-powerful, the Generous, the Creator, the Supreme Lord. . . . He was absorbed in his prayer, but while I was still stooping he opened his eyes. They were so luminous that I felt almost the same awareness of God's presence as in the solitary chapel. This poor of Allah was certainly living with God. Did he see his Face, at least "through a veil"? I thought later on that this meeting, which impressed me deeply, might have been my first form-less call to contemplative life. Often, looking at the gulls, I felt something in me wanting to soar, but much heaviness was pulling me down.

Sometimes we went still farther south to Agadir or to Marrakech, and with the first dunes of the desert there were mirages to enjoy: palm trees mirrored in limpid streams and *dirs* (villages in small oases). The phenomenon had been explained scientifically to me, but it gave me an uncom-fortable sense of the unreliability of my environment.

In spring the plains were like rich, immense carpets of miniature sky-blue irises and bright orange marigolds, some-times hemmed by rows of daffodils. Once I was sent to a summer camp in the southern mountains. It was high and cold there, and I was sick most of the time, but I liked hiking through rocks and dried torrents with other children. Occasionally we met with soldiers of the Foreign Legion keeping the Djebel Toubkal from Mauritanian incursions. One of the legionaries was stung by a large scorpion when we were near his tent. He took a knife from his back pocket and swiftly cut the part of his leg that had been poisoned. A bit of his flesh fell on the ground, and he let the blood flow while he was killing the carapaced spider and laughing at our horrified admiration. These military visits were not allowed by the organizers of the camp, but we managed quite a few escapades.

A more macabre discovery was waiting for us. Some Moslems believe that at their death Allah will pull them up by their hair into paradise. They shave their heads except for a long horse-tail on the top. When they bury their dead, they make shallow graves and leave a handful of hair visible outside the tomb. We children came across such a cemetery, unfortunately when our monitor had had a small accident and had returned to the camp, leaving us with a teenage helper. This young man was very interested in the skulls and other bones, many of them unearthed by rains and jackals. I did not run away as some girls did, but when two boys began playing football with skulls I was shocked and started an argument. They probably just wanted to look smart and tough, but I called them quite a number of "names" and soon had the whole gang against me. I decided to leave the camp and wrote to my parents that I was ill, which was not untrue. They sent a friend to take me down to Marrakech, and this gave me the chance to get more acquainted with this ancient capital of Morocco and enjoy a freedom that I could not have when I was there with my parents.

In this very hot city, life was at its peak just after sunset. I was allowed to roam around the *suks* (market places) and the very large square of Djemaa-el-Fna. There hundreds of small stands lit with oil lamps attracted crowds of men in long white robes and sometimes in *touareg* blue veils, of women completely covered with *haiks*, often leaving only one eye seen and seeing, and of fascinated children. Some people listened for hours to story-tellers from the mountains, sitting on the sand around them and following the cadence of verses with the sway of their bodies. Others looked at the snake charmers fearlessly manipulating reptiles still loaded with venom. You could have a big bowl of steaming rice soup for a few *sous* (cents) and continue your meal with a handful of roasted locusts and some of the fruit that lay in great colorful heaps, figs, melons and bursting pomegranates filled with ruby-like seeds. There were also some political meetings going on and the noise of innumerable bargains.

One day I followed a European man along a street smelling of spices and Indian incense. We entered a large room. Everything around us was flaming red: the walls covered with Moroccan blankets, the altar in the center dressed in scarlet bunting cloth and the carpet of dyed wool on the beaten floor. There was a small inscription dedicating this temple to some Franciscan martyrs who had died there long ago, and I wondered about these followers of my still unknown Father-to-be.

After all these exciting encounters, life at school seemed dull. I do not think that I could have endured the routine and discipline but for the diving thrills, the discovery of the Greek universe of past centuries and the joys of new friendship.

I was still "best friends" with Claudine, and our relationship became somewhat intense and exclusive. I felt that I was losing my interior freedom and deliberately chose another friend, without renouncing the daily sharings and deep mutual understanding that made my conversations with Claudine enriching and pleasant. She agreed that we "adopt" Anne Rival, a fellow student who was also a member of the JEC. Claudine shared with me literary interests, but Anne was a kind of genius in mathematics. She even made me like the logarithm tables. And she had an extraordinary memory. She could recite a page of history after having read it once or twice or recount a small event with all its detailed circumstances years after it happened. Perhaps unfortunately for her, she also had a very vivid affective memory and easily relived the past with all its load of emotion. This I can do, too, though less often and rarely for my comfort. Claudine, whom I briefly described earlier, was a southern type of girl, dark-skinned for a French girl, extrovert, passionate, with black hair and large, very expressive brown eyes. Anne, the daughter of an army colonel who had lost his wife early, was very fair and had innocent blue eyes, a light complexion and wonderful hair. She usually tied it in golden braids that framed her youthful face; but when she let it loose, it fell down to her heels in silky, light-catching waves. My two friends were as different in temperament, gifts and outlook as in appearance. We formed a very united trio but enjoyed the company of other girls as well. Claudine and I were more intense, curious, reading and discussing much with quite independent minds. We loved risk and a full, colorful life. I think we loved God, too, and were ready to sacrifice much for him. It was a time when penance began to make sense to me, and I wish I could have had some guide then. But I never spoke of that. Anne was more traditional and reasonable. She was more studious and not interested in sports and games, but she was not less loving. I trusted her truthfulness and fidelity and admired both her kindness and her talent for resolving all kinds of geometric and arithmetical problems.

In prayer I often felt that now that things were normal at school I should help more at home. I wanted at last to make amends for what I had said to mother on the day she tried to leave us. But she had not been as affected as I thought by my apparent indifference. She said, "I know you wanted me to be free, and it was what I wanted, too; but I am glad that Lucien came for me. You see, I did not desire a child when you came to us, and we are so different." Then she added unexpectedly, "But we can be friends." Maybe this conversation would have further established me in my rejected-child complex if it had taken place two years before, but at thirteen I was more mature. I depended less on what I received from my parents and was more ready to give in return. There was God's gentle insistence, too. Though I still longed for a true mother, and my mother was not the kind of friend I would have chosen, I entered the role. And it worked, in spite of our opposite tendencies and my frequent impatience. We even became fond of each other in a way I could not have thought possible. At the same time, father had seen the danger, and he spent most of his weekends with us, often in some outings or interesting film shows. This was a great improvement in our family life.

Of course mother continued to resent his "political nights" and long absences, but she expressed her feelings less often. We also had our disagreements still, but as long as I let her dress me as she wished, even though I felt disguised, we were indeed good friends. She even insisted that my hair, made stiff by long stays in salty water, should be curled in a permanent wave. Father thought that it was too early to put me into the hands of a hairdresser, and I hated the idea; but one day I made a strong resolution to give in to mother even in that. She triumphantly led me to a fashionable "artist". There I was put under an electric helmet, and I tried to read a magazine during the operation. But soon I called the hairdresser: "It is very hot under here." He answered phlegmatically, "Yes, is it not?" and went to the next customer. I knew I was burning and I said so. He came back with an air that meant, "Of course she is still a child" and exhorted me, "Now, you have to suffer a little if you want to be beautiful." I was rather indifferent to the prospect under the circumstances but not to the paternalistic tone. So I just remained quiet until the end. When they removed the helmet, not only much of my hair but a good part of my scalp left with it. The hairdresser cried out, "But you are all burned. Why did you not say anything?" I did not answer, but I knew that this was my last permanent wave. Though I told mother that I had little pain, it hurt a lot for many days and nights. I sometimes had my picture in sports news, and one of them was taken before my hair had grown again. This provoked astonished reflections and unfavorable comments on my taste and style.

I continued to accompany my father to left-wing meetings, and, with the rise of Fascism in Germany and Italy, they became more violent. One day father was wounded by a stone. Violence repelled me but injustice even more, and I would have risked anything for a chance to build an idealistic new world. My adolescent desires were, however, rather contradictory: besides dedicating my life to working for peace, I wanted to be a Greek scholar, to marry a socialist hero and to die with him on some errand of universal brotherhood. And, above all, to receive the Eucharist. I did not know that soon my future was to be decided, at least in its principal orientation, by our Lady, the Immaculate.

Chapter X

A Threshold

We often set apart a three-week holiday in Europe for "taking a water cure", a fashionable and perhaps useful habit, especially for those who live in the tropics though born in colder climates. Some French towns are known for their mineral waters, which are supposed to work wonders on the liver, joints or heart of those who come to drink from their fonts and enjoy the restful activities, games, pictures and hotel parties that fill their idle days. I liked to play tennis, but being left-handed was a handicap, and many coaches wanted me to use my right hand. I have better recollections of long solitary swims in Lake Geneva amid moving reflections of snowy peaks and swans. But one year, when I was fourteen or fifteen, my father suffered from a sore throat. He had to give up smoking. The doctor suggested that he could replace cigarettes with sweets. Three months later, father showed signs of hyperglycemia and revealed that he was having a good pound of sweets as part of his new daily diet. The doctor preached moderation and sent him for a cure at *Eaux Bonnes* (Good Waters), to drink from a spring that restored health to tired throats. We chose a good hotel, and I found there a band of teenagers already well organized and living quite apart from the middle-aged or old people "in cure", who were their parents and relatives.

The leader of the band, an attractive student about eighteen years old, kissed me the very day we arrived. It was not unpleasant, though I thought he should have asked for my permission. My friend Claudine had begun dating, but I had had no time for such concerns. I knew that my father would object to my flirting with boyfriends, but not my mother. However, our youthful band was more intent upon the exhausting sport of mountain-climbing than on playing around. We (about ten or twelve boys and girls from fifteen to twenty-two years old) went very early in the morning with sandwiches in our pockets, planning carefully our ascent to some sparkling summit. There we enjoyed the splendid view on the chain of peaks, mixed melted snow and chocolate for a drink and returned at sunset very speedily. There were beds of winter streams that were then dry and filled with small boulders and pebbles. We frequently chose a flat stone and threw it on the pebbles, then jumped on it and slid down the torrent bed, all absorbed in the difficult exercise of maintaining our balance on the bumpy path. Only two of us suffered broken bones, which is quite surprising. The beauty of the flowered meadows and of the strangely shaped rocks above them was a continual challenge, and back at the hotel we needed only food (a lot of it) and rest. But on rainy days we played games and chatted. Two of the elders in our group were engaged, and their behavior encouraged freedom among the younger ones. I was caught in some tender manifestations of affection. It never went very far, though it was certainly a little daring for my age and time.

One Sunday my parents decided to visit that center of religious superstition and shameful clerical mercantilism: LOURDES. We arrived early in the morning in the pretty city. I was shocked, of course, by the sale of tasteless religious souvenirs everywhere. My father disappeared into a hotel, where he had found other union leaders, and my mother undertook a visit to the three superimposed churches. I noticed that she never crossed in front of a tabernacle. She would examine the pictures or statues on one side of a church but never went to the other side. I supposed that, from old habit, she could not bring herself to cross without genuflecting, nor, of course, could she give a sign of reverence. Neither did I.

We finally came in front of the Grotto. I did not like the statue, but there was peace there and an atmosphere of fervent prayer. Perhaps there was a Mass at the nearby altar. A priest spoke of the spiritual value of human suffering. In the recurrent murmur of the rosary, I looked up again at the white shape in the rock hole and tried to repeat the unfamiliar words of the Ave Maria (Hail Mary). Suddenly Mary spoke very distinctly in my heart a few perfectly clear words: "You are not meant to marry."

I was astounded. Apart from some silly preadolescent dreams, I had never thought much of marriage yet, but companionship with a man seemed normal. It was just to be expected, and I had never thought of another destiny. Celibacy did not appeal to me. My recent timid experience had been exciting and pleasant. I had never met with a "sister", though perhaps a strange costume in the street made me think that some European women had ways of dressing as strange as any Moslem ones. Even when I heard, or, rather, received these words in my heart, the idea of religious life did not come to my mind; it was too far from my world. But I understood perfectly that our Lady had just forbidden me not only marriage but also, and even more, any kind of complaisance for whoever would pretend to love me. A whole area of life, of pleasure, of experience, intimacy and fruitfulness was suddenly and forever closed to me. I was very conscious of the loss; but something rose in me: a movement of love and trust. My response was wordless and total. There at the feet of the Virgin and consciously into her hands, I surrendered myself to the Lord who was claiming my life. The impression was very strong and left no room for doubt. What is perhaps unusual is that I did not dwell on it or on the consequences of this act. It was done. I would not go back on it, and I do not think that I wondered what kind of future it left me.

In the afternoon we went to the procession of the Blessed Sacrament and the individual blessing of the sick. I saw the Eucharist for the first time and was filled with joy. Mother did not want to leave before the picturesque night candle procession; for the first time also, looking at a multitude of living flames, I heard the Christian Creed. I understood well the Latin words but not all their meaning. I had a feeling of plenitude and certitude, while thousands of voices, pilgrims from Sweden to Brazil, from Australia to Africa, were singing the same Faith. I felt I belonged to it, though I did not believe I could ever be part of the "Catholic Church", that old enemy of justice and peace. Our neighbors on the esplanade were a couple from the United States. They had come all this way for only two days in Mary's city. It might have been the feast of the Assumption, but I knew nothing of the Virgin's feasts. I was to come back to Lourdes as a Poor Clare, very sick and under obedience, to ask for health, and again later on as a representative of contemplative nuns. It would always be a coming home, in my Mother's Garden.

Back in Morocco I continued to keep almost every aspect of my interior life secret even from my closest friends, though both Claudine and Anne would have rejoiced in the knowledge that God now had so great a place in my heart

and life. I had been alone so long in my faith that I was not
able to express it. They were weekly communicants, and
this filled me with envy. There was no perversity in them,
though they were Catholics, and where else could I be
given the Eucharist? I had no access of course to any Eastern
or other Churches.

One Easter day, when the bells were ringing in the spring
air, my longing became too strong to bear. I asked for courage and went to my father. I said to him: "You told me several times that you would leave me free to choose my ways
and my beliefs when I grew up. I want to be instructed in
the Catholic Church." He looked at me, unbelieving. Then
I do not know what came over him. He had never as much
as slapped me after any of my many childish mischiefs, but
then he fell on me and beat me. I was too surprised to react.
I just let him hit me, and I took the blows with a strange
peace in my heart. He broke one lens of my glasses and a bit
of glass entered my eye. I bled profusely. He was stunned
and almost cried. He did not know what to do. Mother was
not there. I told him to call our neighbor, who came immediately. I said that I had fallen on the corner of a table and
broken my glasses. Father was as if lost. I was brought to an
eye surgeon, who after a lengthy examination said that the
glass had stopped one hair's breadth from the pupil. Though
the wound was serious, I was in little danger of losing my
sight. They stitched my cornea, and I was to wear a big
black patch on my eye for several weeks and to avoid swimming and more especially diving. I was forever explaining
how I fell on a table, with my father silent and lamblike at
my side. We never touched on the subject again, but he
knew then and was deeply unhappy because he had hurt me
and because I was not to live by his ideals. I was unhappy,
too, and still spiritually famished.

So one day I went on my bike, far from our place, to a big suburb of Casablanca, the *Roches Noires*, where there was a new granite church. I entered and prayed in front of a marble reproduction of the Sacred Heart of Jesus, the Montmartre statue with open arms, and I went to the priest. I explained that I had been baptized long ago but not instructed in the Faith and had a great desire for the other sacraments, though my parents did not agree. The aging priest, with a kind smile, consented to instruct me and went to fetch some books, but, coming back with them, he asked, "You are not the daughter of Mr. Le Goulard, are you?" I answered that I was. Then his expression changed, and he said, "Oh! I cannot do anything for you, then. Your father can do much harm to the Church." How cowardly! I left him, promising to become a Protestant. But what about the Eucharist?

I was also finding it more and more difficult to understand the difference of behavior between most Moslems and most Christians. Except for a few members of Catholic organizations, Christians, as I saw them, almost never gave evidence of their faith, did not refer to God in their ordinary conversations or allude to him in their public decision-making; and, except for an hour or so on Sundays, they never seemed even to pray. Moslems were constantly, even without engaging in proselytism or making any show of special fervor, making it obvious that God was the Master of all the events of their lives and that they were ever ready to recognize his rights and guidance. They wanted his blessing on their every action; they were consciously dependent on him; they were not ruled by human respect and would not omit to pray several times a day with deep faith and reverence. Our rich acquaintances excused themselves from business or pleasure in a very natural way when it was time for prayer. They were also wont to say, "It is God's will", or to quote the Koran. The Arab who swept our school found it completely normal to spread a small mat in a corner of our courtyard and to prostrate himself in this tiny sacred place in sight of all the girls who were having their recreation around him. He bowed to the ground several times in recollected adoration. Up to now, I do not see why there should be so little of this in Christian practice. One of our maids took us to task one day, saying that, if we did not have the grace of fasting during the Ramadan, at least we should do so during Lent, adding that she did not see fewer Europeans in the bars at this time!

Of course, their faith did not make all Moslems holy. Many were immoral and fanatic. Those who broke the severe one-month fast were put into prison. Two Frenchmen we knew were killed in dramatic circumstances. They wore Arab clothing because they found it cooler than European suits and more dignified than shorts. During the month of Ramadan, they forgot about the fasting and were seen smoking in a market. One Moslem shot them on the spot, mistaking them for coreligionists who scorned the sacred observances. Moslem women were too often mere objects of service or pleasure. Some were even yoked with a donkey or a camel and ploughed the fields with the beast while the husband led the unlikely team. We knew also of some Frenchwomen shut up in stifling harems.

Twice near the holy city of Moulay-Iddriss, we witnessed a band of Ahisauas whirling in a dance not unlike the *mashawe* we see here in Central Africa, but much more violent. They inflicted terrible wounds on themselves with knives and axes. Some dancers collapsed unconscious on the ground, covered with blood. The others leapt over their fallen companions in their trance. We could have been killed for stopping nearby.

I sympathized more with other sides of the Moslem habits or system of values. Though even the poor were almsgivers, most Moslems had no objection to robbing rich people, especially the despised Christians or Europeans. This made it necessary to watch our maids. My father, in conformity with his principles, shrugged his shoulders at the disappearance of food stuffs and even household linen: "They need it more than we do." But mother took another view of the pilfering and tried to enforce high standards of honesty. The maids, however, were quite creative. One of them wore large *saruels*. This is a kind of trousers, very full on top and tied just under the knees. There is ample place for inner pockets in the upper part of the legs. This ingenious woman would never have dared to take great quantities of food from our supplies in one single theft but every day set aside small packets of flour, sugar and such, and had fixed up the lining of her *saruel* with small bottles for oil, wine, milk and liquor. One day she missed a step when climbing down from our veranda to go home, and she fell. She did not break her bones, but she did break her bottles. I went to her rescue and enjoyed the discovery of the forbidden supplies and the silent confusion of the garrulous woman. I would have liked to share the fun with mother but was afraid that under the circumstances she would lose her ordinary sense of humor, and so I kept quiet about the incident. My Arab friend had to go home with a multicolored, tell-tale *saruel*, as I had no such piece of clothing in my wardrobe.

I think I must go back a little, as I remember now some adventures that I forgot to relate.

I have already said that my way to school was short and pleasant, through our street of cottages and a well-kept public garden. I made part of my morning prayer there, a prayer of my own composition, which was probably quite unorthodox. However, each morning I said to the Lord that I was his, and told our Lady that, being unable to bring her flowers of my own, I offered her all the corollas blooming there and in the whole world. One day when I was in these peaceful thoughts I stumbled on a corpse. It was so unexpected that I nearly flew away, but I forced myself to look at the figure on the small path. It was a young man, elegantly dressed, lying on his back with his clothes in perfect order, but his face was very white. There was a small round hole in his forehead and only a trickle of blood on his temple. I found it difficult to touch him to confirm his death. He was cold. I ran to the police station, which was not far away, and came back with the police and Claudine, whom I had met on the way. The young Frenchman was twenty and had been killed by his uncle. The family was rich and the scandal was hushed up.

Another day, almost at the same place, I saw a yellow dog who looked very sad. I cannot resist stray dogs, and usually they cannot resist me either. But my parents would never agree to let me keep them in our backyard. I went to greet and try to cheer the sorrowful animal, but when I patted his head he bit my wrist deeply. When the bleeding stopped, I went to school. My neighbor saw my stained handkerchief, and I told her of my disappointment with the unfriendly dog. I was very displeased when she went to a teacher with the story, but I owe my life to her. The teacher telephoned the police, and they searched for the dog, caught it and had it examined. It died from rabies two days later. The Pasteur clinic was far from our place. The daily shots of infected rabbit marrow made me quite sick during the twenty-one day treatment. My mother, who was by then very attached to me, cried and was very frightened that I would have rabies after all; but I was well again soon after the treatment and, in spite of the difficult bicycle ride on bad roads, did not miss a single school day.

We had greater concerns at the time. My two last years of studies in secondary school were darkened by an enormous approaching cloud. The Second World War was becoming inevitable. We were more conscious of this in my family than most others because of our interest in general politics and my father's connections. For him and for me, too, it was far more threatening than any personal disaster. No illusion or nationalistic enthusiasm could lessen our awareness of a cosmic cataclysm due, not to some inescapable natural accident, but to sheer evil and human madness. I had read horrifying accounts of the soldiers' suffering during the First World War, looked at the monstrous photograph of the *Gueules cassées* (broken faces) and the immense fields of tombs spread from one horizon to the other at the ossuary of Douaumont and of other parts of eastern France. I was fully convinced of the foolishness of a general conflict and of the depths of suffering and distress that it would bring to millions of people for the sake of the sordid interests of the few. I could not stop believing in God, a God of love; but there was an extreme tension in me, and I had no one with whom to discuss the problem of evil or of the Church. My mind was filled with atheistic propaganda, so that scientific Marxist Leninism seemed the only, if extremely unsatisfactory, solution to the problems of human society. I wanted to enter the Communist Party, which I finally did. I was even tempted by ideas of suicide. All this must have been a part of my adolescent crisis as well as the consequence of my training and of the world situation. It was a dark period.

Day after day, and often late into the night, we were studying the reports and predictions and reading all kinds of material on the Third Reich. *Mein Kampf* plunged me into despair, and I could not understand why my companions did not share my impressions.

We also listened to the hysterical voice of Hitler as he rose to power. The Munich agreement of 1938 was not a consolation. Those of my generation who were trying to think felt trapped and powerless against the threat of a kind of universal destruction that many young people also experience today. Besides these anxieties, I deeply shared the distress of Tante Jeanne at the death of her first child and the illness of the other.

With all of this in my mind and heart, I lost much interest in my studies, unless they were linked to some metaphysics or politics, as well as in diving. I was more involved in left-wing movements. My father was an influential member of the Socialist Party but above everything else remained a convinced union leader. He was much solicited both by the Communists and by the Free Masons. My uncle Paul was a "Venerable" in the most important lodge of Africa, but father always declined the invitation to join them, saying, "Both Communists and Masons become like wheels in a mechanism. I do not want to be 'teleguided' but to keep control of my own aims and actions." Though he continually confronted the government representatives in order to obtain better conditions of life for workers and teachers, he won the esteem of his adversaries by his integrity, intelligence and dedication; and he was awarded both the "Academic Palms" for his teaching capacity and the "*Ouissama Alaouite*" (the Moroccan Sultan's distinction) for his service to the country. He never wore these medals any more than he did those he had won during the war. My mother was also elected head of the Union of Post-Telegraph-Telephone workers and filled the office with competence and many sighs. One day father told me, "I know you want to join the Communists. It is all right with me. In fact the best Communists at twenty become the best socialists at forty." He also said, "I cannot understand a young man or woman who is not ready to give his (her) life for a worthwhile ideal." He was no longer a youth, but he was willing to do so still.

The German-Soviet Pact in August 1939 stunned us and our friends. I had already passed the first Baccalaureate and entered the year of philosophy. I had to be separated from my best friends, as Anne went to the boys' college for mathematics and Claudine was ill for some months.

But a new and precious friend was given me: Mademoiselle Martinaggi, our philosophy teacher. Jero (her Christian name is Jeromine) is now in her eighties and still writes to me and sends me books of philosophy and modern magazines. She was then a young woman, physically remarkable as a strong Corsican type. Her complexion was just a shade clearer than the copper skin of a squaw, her nose aquiline, her eyes dark and beautiful. She gathered her black hair in plaits over her ears and wore long, original dresses that we all loved, though our mothers did not. She was full of enthusiasm for most currents of human thought and was herself a Catholic spiritualist of the tendency of Emmanuel Mounier (French Personalism). Mounier had once asked for her hand, and she refused because she was afraid to disappoint him. So she never married. "We must go to the truth with all our heart" (Plato). So I did. How pure the light of Plato seemed to me! But it was to Bergson that I was to remain forever grateful.

There had long been a dichotomy between my faith in God and in the spiritual side of man, on the one hand, and my elaborate Marxist training, on the other. Scientific materialism appeared to be the only logical system of thought, and still I knew that it could not include the deepest truths. Bergson liberated me. His book on memory especially convinced me of the shallowness of materialism and of the fragility of its intellectual foundation. At last I could be whole. The Communist Party still tempted me, but only for its social trends and the heroism of some of its members. I kept my Christian faith secret and enjoyed playing the devil's advocate in discussions and written essays. Miss Martinaggi took great interest in me. She even gave me the key to her flat, and I could always take refuge in her large living room opening onto a palm tree garden. It was a peaceful paradise of books and records. I was a very fast reader but tried, however, to discern and remember, to compare and enrich my personal synthesis. I discovered together and hold in twin loves Claudel and Péguy, Kierkegaard and Berdaieff. For the whole year, I slept little, spoke less with my friends and abandoned the pool. And still there was never time enough. I was already familiar with many poets, painters, sculptors, and now the world of music was open to me. It was a magic world, where you drank ambrosia with semigods like Mozart and Beethoven and escaped for a time the weight of the looming political disasters.

I passed the year's examinations in a kind of daze and total indifference to the results. The teacher of philosophy who examined me during the orals at Rabat, the capital, was known to be a fanatically ascetic Christian. He asked me, "What is the ultimate aim of human life?" I mischievously answered what I did not believe but knew would scandalize him most: "Pleasure." He was fully roused. "Pleasure?" We began a very spirited discussion, which soon attracted a small crowd of interested listeners around us (the orals were public). I defended the hedonistic theories with great firmness, and I knew my authors from Epicurus to Bentham. He was mean enough to give me a low mark, which attracted unfavorable comments on his fairness. But my marks for the written part of the examination were too high for failure. Anyway I had had my little fun, and my parents were very proud of me, though there was little reason for it. They gave me my first stone, a burnt topaz ring, and a box of honeyed cigarettes, signs of adulthood.

Some days later I received the "Great Prizes" both for literature and for philosophy. It would have meant something two years earlier, but in 1939 such successes looked derisive.

To be adolescent then was to be prepared to become "flesh for bullets", to indulge in cheap pleasures in order to forget the future or to become vaguely suicidal or anarchist. In Morocco, hashish, opium and hemp were also available in my milieu, though European students had not yet tasted this "way out", but I remembered the forbidden cupboard and the shadow over me, and, even when devoured with curiosity, I never touched a drug of this kind.

The ending of the Spanish war under Franquist rule left many of us very bitter, too.

Some students of course were filled with bellicose dreams. I believe it was not through lack of courage that many young Frenchmen yielded too soon to Hitler's invasion. It was lack of motivation, of trust in their governments and in the right to fight modern wars. And they were upon us. If I had been in France, I could have done what so many did, Christians and Communists united for a time: they let the Germans take over their country, thinking that these enemies were still possible brothers and that no evil was greater than the evil of war. But experiencing the slavery of

Nazi occupation or the horrors of death camps, they turned to the maquis and Resistance fighting.

We went to France for our last European holiday. I don't remember anything except wondering why there was still so little awareness in many groups and families of the scope and proximity of danger. Few perhaps spent such long hours analyzing the news. It was with little hope of a joyful return that we left our dear ones and our country to begin our journey back to Morocco.

At the end of August, I was with my mother at Marseilles, waiting for the boat. Father had gone already, under threat of a sudden mobilization. Mother was very anxious because he had said that he would never take arms again, and conscientious objectors in time of war could be executed, although that is not the case now. On August 31, in the evening, we were called to look at the sea. It was completely red. I had never seen it this color. It was not even sunset yet; the sky was also reddish, but the sea was like a sea of blood, without any change of hue as far as the horizon. I tried to think of some scientific explanation, which should have been easy to find, but under the circumstances, it did seem to be a portent. People on the quays looked on, silent and frightened. A small passenger liner took us the following day.

At first we had a peaceful journey, and I made friends with young Italians who kept their spirits up with songs and dances. On September 3, a radio message informed us that we were at war with the Axis, and the Italians on board immediately became our "enemies". They were consequently thrown into a kind of prison. The absurdity of it all revolted me, but I had to comfort my mother and so abstained from useless comments. I had an almost protective love for her. She had a vivid imagination and already saw my father shot. The next radio message said that a German submarine had been detected not very far from us. We sped off to the Spanish port of Cartagena. Spain was quite hostile, too. We spent two or three days in a blue bay, with little food and even less to cheer us. When we took to sea again, it was under the supposed threat of an air attack, and just to reach Casablanca seemed quite an achievement.

To our great relief, we found my father in the uniform of a sergeant-major (his rank from the last war). He had been given a job he could handle without problems of conscience: to supervise the distribution of food supplies in the barracks. His friend Jean Tanguy, who was always spruce even in a hunting suit, was walking despondently in baggy trousers and a shirt too narrow for his broad shoulders. Another of our friends was busy proclaiming his pacifist views and risking prison for refusing to hold a rifle, but, when he heard that his native Corsica had been attacked, he volunteered to fight. One of my teachers, a perfect intellectual, was given a bridge to defend, but fortunately there was no enemy. The "phony war" had begun. Poland was lost after Czechoslovakia and Austria, and war was declared, but nobody moved for months.

Then in a few weeks of anguish and despair, France was invaded and defeated. A hated armistice was signed by Pétain. Brittany was behind a kind of "iron curtain".

In October 1940, it was decided that I would go to Algiers, as French universities were inaccessible then. I convinced Anne that it was the best for her, too, and Claudine began a year of propaedeutics in Rabat.

I found it difficult to leave my parents behind, knowing that my father was not safe under the new regime.

Chapter XI

Student in Algiers

I traveled with Anne from Casablanca to Algiers by train. There we enrolled in the University, she for a degree in differential calculus and I in philosophy. While attending all the lectures in philosophy, I decided to prepare also for a degree in literature and another one in psychology. It seemed enough work for the first year. But it proved to be the smallest part of my activities.

From the start I wanted to find the Church where I could finally be at home and to take my place in the adult Communist Party. I did not see any difficulty in belonging to both, and I was a cardbearer in the Party before I could be sure of becoming a Catholic for good. The Party was already preparing for the independence of Algeria, and this was something I was determined to help in, even if my contribution had to be very small. Besides, I did not want to be immersed in the bourgeois, high-class group of university students in a colonized country.

The University of Algiers was built in a rather nineteenth-century style but had good facilities: large amphitheaters, a well-equipped medical faculty, a rich library. The Algerians burned this library before independence. It contained hundreds of thousands of books, many of them rare specimens. The botanical garden was very small but well tended. Under the multishaped palm trees and other forms of tropical vegetation, we could exchange notes, ideas and forbidden political views. There were also, of course, some romantic encounters under the cocoa leaves or the giant hibiscus flowers. Extra staff had been called from France to respond to the needs of a swollen number of students, who would normally have gone to Paris or Bordeaux. Most of these were French, but there were Arabs, too, and some black students. I never noticed signs of racial tension until, after the Germans invaded France, the Vichy government imposed a ban on Jews. Many students whom we could not even distinguish from the others by any exterior sign, bright young people, often of the same culture and religion as the others, were found to have a grandmother or a great-grandfather with a bit of Jewish blood and were expelled. Some, deported, were to end in torture and misery. Our black fellow students were also subjected to some humiliating checks, but we closed ranks with them. After all, we were in Africa. The Pétain administration was too afraid of troubles in North Africa to impose there all the Nazi-inspired laws that they tried to enforce in Europe.

There were clashes between our left-wing and right-wing professors. Sometimes they did not restrict themselves to words. But almost all of them were competent, sometimes creative and generally dedicated intellectuals. In literature I found myself listening to Mr. Busson, a former priest who had renounced his priesthood because his bishop had vetoed his publishing a cherished but slightly heretical thesis. He was thin, subtle and tormented and was married to a large, vulgar and placid woman. She was never seen out of their home, and I was to be one of the very few students (he had almost two hundred listeners at his university lectures) ever invited there. This came about because some indiscreet friend gave him a few poems I had written. One day he summoned me to an interview that left me forever doubtful of literary criticism. What I heard in his stuffy library, with his wife pouring out sweetish coffee in tiny cups and all the windows shut against the clear skies, was a perfect but amazing lecture on what I had written quite accidentally in a moment of juvenile expansiveness. The comments were bright and on the whole encouraging. I learned how these few pages had been inspired and composed, in which state of mind and soul I was at the time they were written and whose influence had made me choose this expression or use that metaphor. It was very clever, interesting and plausible. But none of it was true. I had never read most of the authors who were supposed to have influenced me. My aims and feelings were vastly different from what Busson described with convincing skill. I tried to protest but was no more heard than the dead authors who are the usual victims of these brilliant expositions.

Our Latin professor had nothing to excite mind or imagination, and to me the dullest part of the program was the study of a rather licentious Roman poet of the first century B.C., Ovid. I crossed him off my own program. Fate decreed that, at the oral of the end-of-year examination, I was questioned only on his *Metamorphoses* for the Latin part. I honestly said that I had never opened this book and was rewarded with a round zero. This was disqualifying, for a student with a zero in any subject failed the whole examination. But the other professors, especially Busson, who believed in my literary career, said that it was "unthinkable" to deny me the degree for having overlooked one book of one author. They asked the professor concerned to give me half (out of twenty) instead of zero. He agreed. As my other marks were more than compensatory, I received my degree in classical literature without becoming Ovidian.

In psychology it went more smoothly. I spent many happy nights (I was otherwise busy during the days, as I will explain later on) on Freud and the mysteries of our unconscious, making experiments with my friends and studying Dalbiez.

Besides this, I followed all the lectures and did the readings in general philosophy for three years. Our professor, P. Mesnard, was a right-wing Catholic with a deep-rooted dislike for Saint Thomas. He fed us with the dry bread of scholarly commentaries on Descartes' *Discourse on the Method of Rightly Conducting the Reason.* The following year it was on the *Critique of Pure Reason* of Immanuel Kant. And the third one was dedicated to Leibnitz and Spinoza; quite a bit of abstract art, though I rather enjoyed it, but much more *The Dark Night of the Soul* of Saint John of the Cross, which was unexpectedly thrown in. It was my first contact with mysticism. I added both Saint Teresa and Saint Angela of Foligno in the dazzling Hello translation to my nocturnal delights. To finish with my studies, I also passed a third "certificate" of moral science (mainly in Aristotle) and sociology (Durkheim). We were going to the Dominicans for glimpses of Saint Thomas. This infuriated our professor and gave some life to our discussions. Mesnard knew that I was in the Communist Party, and it worried him. He, too, invited me several times to his home, though I had the great drawback of not playing bridge. As he sometimes indulged in matchmaking, I noticed that there was always only one male student, and always the same one, invited with me. Our professor used to speak highly of the other to each of us. He was clearly disappointed when I told him that, though I appreciated his choice of a partner for me, I was not interested in marrying any of his young philosophers. I remember my last encounter with my undeclared suitor better than all the others. It was a short time before I followed my call to the cloister and he to his delayed mobilization. I had written to him that I wanted to be a Poor Clare. He caught sight of me in a bus and jumped on the platform, but he could not reach me because the bus was filled with tightly packed passengers. So he shouted over half a hundred heads, "Hi, Luce, do not enter that monastery. You are not strong enough for that life. They will kill you there." I blushed and shook my head at him angrily. But he shouted even louder, "Or you will kill your superiors!" And having let fly this Parthian shaft, he waved and jumped down on the street. I left the bus rather hastily, too.

But I am anticipating. Though I enjoyed my studies and continued to read a great deal, my side activities took more and more of my days; and during the last year I was caught up in an adventure that could only have happened in time of revolution or war. It left me no time or energy for anything more.

I should also say something here of my involvement with and in the Communist Party, which was then underground. I will not come back to the subject, and I do not intend to treat it extensively. Discretion once promised has to be observed even when changed circumstances render disclosures of little consequence. Though some intellectuals of the Party wanted students with them, I asked to be integrated in a cell where a team of Arab and French workers were collaborating. Our leader was a docker, though he did not look strong. He impressed on us continually that we had to be Communists not only in our political struggle but in our whole life. Discipline was strict, militancy fervent. We had a weekly meeting where we were each given some assignment: to bring people to Soviet films, to glue a poster on town walls or to watch (and fight if necessary) to see that it was not torn off, to obtain or transmit information, to beg in the streets for the International Red Relief Fund or to work more directly for some project linked to the "Preparation for Algerian Independence". At the next meeting, we had to give an account of our task to the whole group, which discussed it, or to the leader, who helped us to criticize our own achievements so that the praxis of each member might be better adapted to the aims of the Party. This was a practical, effective, continuous formation. At the grassroots level, I met with much dedication and generosity in the Party but also with violence and hatred. Cunning was more frequent at higher levels of this hierarchized society, and I was still naïve. The Gulag was very far from our thoughts and perspectives.

One little incident remains very clear in my memory. Before the arrival of the Allies in North Africa, we suffered from food restrictions. We could obtain very little meat, fish or dairy products and were given lots of rutabagas (watery roots) instead of potatoes. One day I visited a wealthy friend. Her parents had a big farm as well as a large town house. When I entered their luxurious dining room, they were having tea. It did not escape me that her mother, as soon as she saw me, hid a large butter dish in her sideboard. This was a very Christian lady. The same day, in the late evening, I had to give a message to a Communist laborer. He was alone, sitting on a big box and eating on an upturned case. His evening meal consisted only of a hunk of bread and a piece of cheese. Cheese in those times was difficult to find. He pushed it immediately toward me with a smile, "Welcome, comrade! Help me with this. Youth has a good appetite."

When I became a Catholic, the students' chaplain told me that I should see the Vicar General about my adherence to the Party. I told the Vicar that I could not understand why I should leave it. He looked quite frightened. It was finally decided that I would consult the chaplain of the Young Catholic Workers (JEC) in case of conflict between my allegiances. So I went to Father Andrew Brazzola, a young and saintly priest with a dynamic faith, experience of the Workers' culture and a sense of humor. He let me do everything required of me until I was promoted "Revolutionary Agitator" at the University. Then he told me that I should find a pretext to decline the responsibility because I could be manipulated. He knew, too, that under the circumstances I risked prison. I refused this particular assignment but remained in the Party to the end, though I lost some illusions on the way.

I was to enjoy the cultural refinement of some of my wealthy friends and acquaintances, but I felt a deeper sense of solidarity with my comrades and was never ill at ease with them. With them I never felt, either, that being a girl or a woman was a sad defect and that we had to be distrusted and reduced to total dependence on male government in all domains. I was not used to this mentality. And yet there was a dimension of truth and life that was also missing in the Party, and I experienced there other kinds of intolerance. My comrades, however, accepted quite well my Christian idiosyncrasy, thinking that it would pass away with a bit more knowledge, experience and maturity. So we remained together. When I entered the monastery as a postulant, Mother Portress examined my papers and discovered my Party card, with the stamps of recent months. She ran to the abbess, holding it as if it were on fire. However, the abbess already knew, and I had just resigned from my office in the social services of the De Gaulle government. Gaullists and Communists were dying together in France for the liberation of their country.

Chapter XII

The Search

It is time now to come back to my first weeks in Algiers and my search for a spiritual home. It is almost impossible for a born Catholic to understand the problems and sufferings of some converts. Many come from prejudice; but there are some prejudices that are just an exaggeration of the truth and are therefore very hard to disprove. Some also come from environment and culture and have very deep roots and emotional content.

For my people and myself, the Catholic Church was the Church of the Inquisition and the Borgias, cruel, sly and ambitious, the Church that fights for power at any price and enslaves even consciences. It was not only hatred that all this engendered but disgust, as subnormal human vices do. One day in Spain we visited a cathedral, and I saw big, ugly boxes on the sides. I asked what they were. A friend of my father answered, "This is the hidden place where a priest exercises his concealed power on minds and hearts." These words and many others had made Catholicism very repugnant to me. I thought that my friends were good in spite of, not because of, their Catholic upbringing.

When I began to go to Mass, I was constantly bewildered and shocked. Why put a Host in the open mouth of an adult? Why kneel down at Christmas before a set of plaster

statues? Why dress a man in what seemed to me bridal
finery to say Mass? I have spoken already about the fact that
women were often treated as minors there. There was a lot
of bourgeois moralizing in sermons and little about Jesus,
and also little about the heroic behavior that my naïve youth
was expecting. And one day I watched a crowd of people
kneeling in front of a banner that revolted me. I saw it only
as a mass of flesh dripping blood. I was told it was the Sacred
Heart. I found it distasteful to use "heart" for a person and
strange to use "sacred", which I heard when people were
swearing. I had to read Foucauld and Teilhard before I
understood and accepted this symbol. When it was first proposed to me, I only felt that I did not even speak the same
language as these French Catholic people. Many of the
issues, big and small, that tormented me then have been and
are still openly discussed in the Church, most of them on
both a theological and a cultural level. When, just before Vatican II, I was sent to Central Africa to implant Saint Clare's
monastic and Franciscan life, my past experience made me
sensitive to this essential missionary problem: how to present
the Gospel and the Christian traditions without imposing
cultural expressions that have nothing to do with the real
content of the message.

I turned to Protestantism and visited a number of sects. I
was eagerly received but met with even more problems
there. For instance, after all that Christ had said about the
Sabbath being for man, what was the meaning of all this
witnessing about the sacrifice of jobs and schooling to maintain Saturday as a holy day? And none of them had the
Eucharist.

The Eucharist alone brought me, very unwillingly, to the
threshold of the Catholic Church; and only after this threshold was passed did I discover the other riches inside. It was a

painful "passover" and a rupture with my own world. My parents could not interfere now, but they would suffer intensely if I chose to belong to the Catholic Church. This I wanted to avoid. I was writing to them almost every day and sharing much of my life with them. A "conversion" would also be very untimely when my father was at great risk of being imprisoned or even perhaps executed by a government (Pétain) that was spurned in our milieu and that favored a return to traditional religious values. In fact, what I feared did happen. As soon as it was known that I was "going to Mass", my father's enemies in his own Party said, "He sends his daughter to church in order to be on better terms with the Vichy administration." Of course this hurt him very much. Some of our best friends refused to open their doors to me. But this was not the worst: the fight was inside me. Christmas found me undecided. I was regularly going to the meetings and Masses of the JEC, and in January the Association held elections to some responsible positions. I was elected chairwoman for the philosophy group and went immediately to the chaplain to explain that I could not accept as I was not a Catholic. He listened and said: "You have been elected and you have been baptized. You manifest a strong faith and should accept." When I complained to Anne that he did not know me, she answered quizzically, "Oh! he knows you enough to prefer having you with him than against him." Of course I did not tell my companions that I was in the Communist Party, as it was under interdict and membership was secret. I remained in the JEC, feeling more at ease among the students than in any other Catholic group.

We had a day of retreat with a refugee Alsatian prelate who was giving conferences at a Catholic girls' college. Commenting on a thought of Father de Foucauld, he told us something like this: "The essence of love is desire. We should desire one thing so much that the rest does not count for us. To sacrifice our love except for a higher love is foolish and harmful. Those who sacrifice everything for their essential love are the only ones who reach union with God." I prayed one hour on this and went to the prelate, asking him to hear my confession. I told him that perhaps I would not be able to speak to him in the "box", and he took me to a private room. Then I went as honestly as I could over my sins. But he asked me questions about my spiritual life that I discovered I could not answer. A source of deep suffering began then to surface. I had been alone so long in my life with God that I could not express it. What I write here is still partly unknown to my dearest friends of the time. It is only in recent years that I have been able to relate something of past spiritual experiences. Even during my religious life, though often sharing on many subjects related to faith, I kept the "secret of the King" but was often imprisoned in myself and unable to prevent misunderstandings from arising.

So, this priest asked why I came to the Church, and I answered that I wanted the Eucharist, but I could not explain "who told me about the sacraments". Besides, I had a great contrition for all that I had done that was unkind; but he was mostly interested in my larceny. He wanted me to say how many times and how much I had stolen. I tried to guess and gave an exaggerated sum. Then he said that "restitution" was necessary. Finally, when he proposed that I give the supposedly stolen money to the poor, I promised to do so. I received the absolution with great anxiety: I could work for money, but should I pay for everything before receiving the Eucharist? I did not dare ask the priest, but he himself concluded, "Come here tomorrow for your first

Communion. It is the feast of the Purification of our Lady. The sisters and the girls will sing for you." I was horrified and said the first thing that came to my mind. "Oh, no, thank you, Monsignor, I prefer it to be very discreet, and the chaplain of the students wants it done at their Mass." I escaped in a state of interior turmoil: I had told a lie, and just after my first confession! What was the use, then, of this confession, and was it sacrilegious? I spent the night in these perplexities.

The following day I climbed the hill of Our Lady of Africa with Anne and other students to attend the solemn vows of our chaplain, Father Pignal, in the Jesuits' residence. Crowds, candles, songs . . . and Communion. But not for me. I was still filled with doubts and remorse. The day was clear. The sea viewed from the hill was all blue and silver under the young sun of February. I found respite in the basilica and some courage to speak to Father Pignal, who for a time was greatly improved by his retreat and vows. I told him that I had gone to confession but that I had spoiled the whole thing by saying he wanted me to receive Communion in the students' chapel though he did not even know about it. But he laughed. "This was an implicit truth. Do come next Wednesday." I asked him to keep it quiet, and I did not speak to anyone except Anne about this first Communion. It took place at a JEC Mass. I went to my Lord. At last. More than anything else on earth I wanted to meet him, but unconsciously I was also expecting that this would be a moving event. So it surprised me that, instead, it stilled me. As soon as the Host was secure in me and I was back on my bench, this stillness penetrated me. Even physically I could not move. At the same time the touch was so light, the heart so gently held, that maybe this unknown Presence-filled silence, this attentive stillness was necessary in order to

perceive the Lord's Eucharistic Gift. To speak of this is to try
to reconstruct a cloud with bricks. For many years to come I
was to be always invaded by this stillness reorienting my
whole being toward Christ when I received the Eucharist. I
thought that this was the effect of all Communions. How
could I have known that God has as many ways to come as
he has children, and even more? When I read that Teresa
Neuman was able to discern a consecrated Host from a non-
consecrated one when receiving it, I was perplexed. How
was it possible *not* to discern the tasteless bread from the
Lord of Peace? I asked the chaplain, who looked suspiciously
at me and said, "Now, what is that? Don't try to be funny." It
certainly did not encourage me to openness, though I was in
great need of guidance and also of filling all the gaps in my
Christian education. But nobody saw this need, because I
had a more extensive knowledge of theology than other
young people. And though I felt it myself, I did not know
what to ask.

I was told to go to confession twice a month if I wanted
to receive the Eucharist often. I went to any church that
happened to be close to where I was on Saturdays. One day,
a confessor asked, "Are you not a student? "

"I am."

"Are you studying seriously? "

"I do some studies, but these two weeks I could not. I
have had more important things to do."

He interrupted me angrily. "Nothing is more important
than duty, and your first duty is to mind your books." I tried
to explain that I was also teaching, and so on, but he was full
of his subject and added, "You should not argue with a
priest when you go to confession. God wants a spirit of faith
and obedience." This was the end! The trouble was that I
did have some spirit of faith, but it was still unenlightened. I

took this literally. It only led me to painful confusion, especially in my early religious life.

Sometime before this incident, Professor Mesnard had
summoned me to announce, "The principal of a private college has lost his teacher of philosophy through mobilization.
Replace him. I selected you, and I am sure you can do well."
Of course I objected that I was not prepared. But it was
wartime; many women were doing, and often doing far better than expected, what they were not qualified to do; and I
had promised "restitution". It was a well-paid job for only a
few hours a week. These rich students had a peculiarity that
made them less acceptable to prospective teachers: each one
of them, boys and girls, had been dismissed from other
schools for bad conduct, indiscipline, drug offenses, and so
forth. When I went to Paris in 1983, one of them made a
journey of six hundred kilometers to meet me for half an
hour and said, "The little faith I still have comes from your
course on the meaning of life." I have no memory of it, but I
remember well these students about my own age with a reputation for "incorrigibility", and how I loved them! They
responded to this, and I had to find my way between too
much and not enough proximity. I do not think I have ever
done anything in my life to attract or attach anybody to
myself, at least purposely. Even then I wanted them to be
whole and to belong to Christ, who could heal them, and I
did not yield to their demands on my time and attention
when I felt it made them dependent on me. It was a struggle, though, because some of them were possessive. Nine out
of eleven succeeded in their examinations at the end of the
year. It was a high rate for this kind of school. I was only one
of the teachers there, of course, but I was very happy,
because for most of these youngsters this success was a way
out of a more and more marginalized life. When that

dictatorial confessor scolded me, I had given them a whole
week for reviewing their program with me. Normally I also
passed my own examinations, except the last year; and I was
faithful to daily Mass and mental prayer. I must admit, however, that I was sometimes far from discerning the hierarchy
of duties and was often overstretched and exhausted.

The only priest that I felt did understand me, though I
spoke little of myself even to him, was a young, bright,
vibrant refugee who lived in a toolshed. This was l'Abbé
Eberhard, a Swiss priest who has since founded a famous
retreat house at Poissy, near Paris. And there was also the
odd, aging parish pastor of the Spanish colony in Algiers,
Father Esquerro. One day he told me in his broken French,
"You are always anxious. Your love is imperfect, not because
of what you have just said, but because you feel that your
anxiety is more holy than the peace of Jesus." The lesson
struck me, but it took me many years to learn it practically, if
I ever did. This little man of God was loved by the poor but
considered eccentric by his colleagues. The Archbishop
asked the Jesuits to invite him to their table for daily lunch
because he was living like the Curé d'Ars on rotten potatoes. One day he went to the post office in his threadbare
cassock and ragged round hat to buy stamps, and he had to
wait a long time. When he reached the small window, he
gazed distractedly at the pretty employee and burst out quite
loudly: "*Yo te amo, oh, cuanto te amo!*" ("I love you, oh, how I
love you!") The young woman blushed (French people can
understand this kind of Spanish) and protested, "How can
you? . . . and you a priest!" It is fortunate that a man in the
queue knew him and exclaimed, "No harm, lady; he is
speaking to Jesus!"

Some of the students asked him to teach us mental prayer,
and he began, but he had to return to Spain very suddenly.

He had naïvely hidden some compatriots from the police, and his friends organized his escape before he could be taken to prison. He had only tropical sandals on his feet, and one of them fell off when he was rushed into a small plane. So it happened that he arrived in Spain half barefoot, and we kept a worn-out sandal as a relic and lost a wise counselor with a reputation for near-madness.

I turned more than ever to my friends for my initiation into Christian life.

Chapter XIII

More about Friends
and about the Casbah

How blessed I am and always have been in my friends! They have been extremely faithful and generous to me and have forgiven me seventy times seven for being impatient and for demanding from them the perfection that I am so far from possessing. Of course there are many degrees of intimacy. If it is a question of opening one's heart completely to a beloved "other" and wanting to be with him continually, I have had only one friend: Jesus, the Christ. But in him I have met many who enriched me greatly. With a few I am deeply united in him. We have to go through storms and nights before finding such unity: searching for the essential through contrasting cultures, characters, generations, backgrounds. Yet how solid the relationship and mutual trust are after such a journey, my dear abbess here in Zambia, Mother Josefa, knows well. When the great-grandchildren of Breton sailors and of Zulu warriors meet, we may expect some struggle before perfect mutual understanding and union may be realized. There were also differences of culture among my wartime friends. I have spoken already of Claudine and Anne, to whom I owe my Christian initiation. I was given the sacrament of Confirmation in June 1941, and, fittingly,

Anne was my sponsor. I am moved each time I think of all I received from my friends, and I smile when I see those who are "cohabiting" in my heart. Some would perhaps not get along so well in other meeting places: an English artist sister who taught me the demands of truth in our whole life, a Malawian mother who showed me how love grows on suffering, an Indian farmer God gave me as a brother here in Zambia and who opened to me the riches of the Bhagavad-Gita, missionaries here, families in Paris and Canada, Poor Clares in Africa, France and the United States. Of course there are different levels of communication, but what a grace to be able to find such variety in the gifts, such generosity in the sharing and such possibilities of deep relationship in our own Franciscan communities. If I were to speak of my sisters here and in Algiers and Lilongwe, could I ever finish? It is not my purpose in this book, and I am again going too much ahead in space and time.

When I left my story, I only wanted to introduce one new friend, Claire Cauthier, usually called "Lélou", and now Mme. Costa-Marini. Her parents were acquaintances of Anne's relatives, and she was studying English literature. There was flame and tenderness in her, passion and silence. She was suffering intensely both on her own account and on her mother's and sister's from a difficult family situation. Her uncle had been, I believe, the last French Governor of Vietnam, where Lélou had also lived. I liked the lacquer panels and other art objects they had brought from the Far East and that looked so foreign in this Algerian city. My friend was and still is among the rich but remarkably free from attachment and vanity.

She had a beautiful voice and sang a solo for the marriage of her sister. I do not remember what kind of religious music it was, but her voice filled the vast church with easy, golden waves. She herself was hidden. Because it was a wedding, I thought of Cana and Mary. For the first time, the power of intercession appeared to me to be filling the whole church, answering every need, but coming only through hidden sources of love. Could I become such a source? The song ceased, but the impression remained.

I should also speak of Anne-Marie Baron, but then let us go and meet her in the Casbah, where I was to spend far more time than in the University buildings.

This part of Algiers is on the shore of the Mediterranean Sea, pressing against the vast city but different and shut in on itself. Its hundreds of tiny dwellings heaped on the hillside look white and compact from afar. From inside, it is an immense maze of very narrow streets, climbing up and down, twisting twenty or more times, ending suddenly or opening unexpectedly into a courtyard or a similar, crowded road. It has certainly much in common with the *favelas* of São Paulo or the slums of Genoa, but the houses here are not made of tin and cardboard. They were built with adobe long ago and sometimes now in whitewashed cement blocks. The roofs usually leak but are terraced, and you can jump from one house to another on these flat tops as surely as down on the slimy streets encumbered with small, patient donkeys, vociferous urchins and veiled women. What makes the difference is also the Islamic world, the eight hundred years of inhabitation (our Western slums are quite recent) and the extremely corrupt environment, at least in some parts, at the time we visited this astonishing area.

The Casbah has been famous for centuries for the large number and diversity of its brothels, opium houses and shadowy businesses. Large fortunes were passing from hand to hand there, but most of the population lived in extreme misery; hard-working people rubbed shoulders with drug traffickers, and women fought for the doubtful survival of their children in accepted or despised ways. I have no statistics and can only make a rough guess that at least one hundred thousand people were living there during the war in subhuman conditions.

Anne-Marie Baron was a student in philosophy who had already obtained her Master of Arts diploma and was preparing a sociology thesis for which she needed much information from the Casbah, especially on mixed marriages. For help and guidance, she went to the White Fathers who had their house on the edge of the Casbah and were the only missionaries interested in this underworld. A learned and dedicated priest gave her addresses of people to visit, academic counseling and access to the precious map of the Casbah without which she would have gotten lost more surely than Theseus in the Labyrinth. Anne-Marie was from a rich merchant family; and her uncle, Monsignor Baron, a convert of Léon Bloy, had a great influence in and outside the circle of her relatives. She had had very little contact with misery and was appalled by what she saw in the Casbah. She began visiting some needy women, more out of compassion than for her original purpose. I met her at Mesnard's courses and accompanied her on some visits, then asked my friends to help.

When Father Letellier saw that some organization was needed for this work, we formed ESSANA (Team for Social Service and Friendship in North Africa). The aim of the team was to become close to the poor and offer all the help we could in affection, time and, when required, information about jobs and so on, or distribution of urgent supplies provided by some religious congregations. The students dedicated half a day each week to this service and had "their" families, as in our estimation the quality of relationship had more value than the sharing of goods. Anne-Marie was a full-time worker, though still gathering information for her thesis. And I became more and more involved in this activity under the creative but somewhat unwise guidance of Father Letellier. He soon thought of founding a new congregation. It was said afterward that I consented to be a keystone in the project, then withdrew, ruining it and perhaps the religious "vocation" of Anne-Marie. The truth is that I never said Yes or No, because I was very conscious of already belonging to Christ, and so I waited for my Lord to take some initiative. Having no sign or insight concerning this plan, his will or my future, I just tried to be completely available for the time when he would decide. Maybe I should have expressed at least this indecision. However, it was taken for granted that "Qui ne dit mot, consent." I was not aware that I would disappoint others by following another path.

The rules of ESSANA specified that we should go through the Casbah only in twos, but there were so many people to visit that Anne-Marie and I often went alone. We also kept the most dangerous parts for ourselves. It was very easy to wring "permissions" for daring adventures from Father Letellier, and when he was mobilized we were on our own.

There, too, we made friends in spite of the great differences in cultures, ways of life and creeds. Anne (now Sister Agnes) is still in correspondence with some, but most of them were illiterate, though Mr. Sebti, a very convinced Moslem, proved to be quite a scholar and tried repeatedly to convert me. He lent me books explaining away the death of Jesus (it was Judas of course who was crucified, not the great Prophet that Christians misunderstood).

Anne-Marie and I did not share all our adventures with the other members of the team. We even spent nights in the

Casbah. We happened to be caught in police raids and brought to the station. Once we slept in a crowded hovel on an infested mat. Another day we were invited, again during the night, to a traditional marriage feast, this time by one of the rare well-to-do families still dwelling in the district. We were led to the second floor of a large house to greet the bride. She had already been sitting for long hours on a stiff wooden chair, dutifully crying. When she had no tears left, some gold and silver ones were glued on her amber-colored cheeks. From time to time, she withdrew to change her dress, as she had to show all her dowry and the gifts of the bridegroom. We could address her, but she had to keep perfect silence. It was said that she had never seen her fiancé; but even that night, when the men began dancing among themselves in the illuminated patio, we saw the ladies laughing on the interior veranda and peeping down through tiny holes cut in the heavy curtains. We had also heard Moslem girls saying, "We cannot choose our first husband, but we shall choose the second one." The divorce rate was high, especially among the educated young women. We were given heaps of spiced or sweet food. Then the night procession began. Many of us had oil lamps in our hands, and it was impossible not to think of the Parable of the Ten Virgins, especially when we met the bridegroom's procession coming to take possession of the bride. She was lifted up over the threshold of her new house and her face unveiled. She shared orange-blossom water with the bridegroom, and we all drank from the same cup. Almost always we were the only Christians there, but we never met with the fanaticism I had known in Morocco.

Such festive occasions were rare. What we had to deal with was suffering and vice bred of misery. I do not like to recall it and will only go through a few flashes.

Late afternoon in a very small room, whitewashed but dirty. Today I have a companion, and we have stopped at this house to get news of a sick child. The other children leave us to fetch their mother. We hear a kind of moan, very close to us. There is a cupboard in the thick wall of dried mud, and the voice seems to come from there. I open it: on the shelf is a very old, shriveled woman, like a heap of darkened bones in a rag. But somehow the bones move. The children come back with their mother. No one looks surprised. We ask for an explanation, while we gather the old woman in our arms and lay her down on a sack. The younger woman says calmly, "It is grandma. We are seven to sleep here every night, and, even tightly packed as we are, there is not room enough, so we put her in the cupboard. But with the child so sick I forgot her this morning, and one of the toddlers must have pushed the door."

In another house a man is dying in a pool of blood and his two wives scream. It must be a case of T.B. hemoptysis. There is always much humidity in this kind of room. Very like a burial vault, it is under the level of the street and without opening except a small door into another room. We have the whole family checked up: three adults and five children suffer from T.B.

For six months I was alone, "in charge" of visiting some poor but normal families in the very heart of the famous prostitutes' ward, the *quartier réservé* of Algiers. On each of the rare houses not occupied by one of the more than a hundred brothels, there was the painted label *Maison honnête* ("Decent/Honest house"). I had to go along these streets with small open rooms on each side with ladies-for-sale in bikinis on show on their threshold. I do not know why most of them, even in summer, had ankle socks on, though no dress. Some were pretty, some very ugly; and prices varied accordingly. When there were many men around I was afraid; but though I was not supposed to try, I wanted to speak to these women in the hope that some, being detained there through deceit or through force, would be willing to escape with some help. I made a plan and went one day, very decided to establish some first contacts.

That morning, as soon as I arrived, a young, perhaps beautiful, but much-painted woman put on a blouse and came to me across the street. She said kindly, "My girl, this is not a place for you. You are around too often and will be caught by one of our pimps or customers. Let some old woman do your work, whatever it is." She was smiling, but how rebuked and humiliated I felt: I was not the rescuer but the one rescued! I thanked her, blushing from the revelation of my foolishness. I do believe she will precede me in paradise. A young priest who had lost his way was also exhorted to prudence, though insulted by some other dwellers in bikinis. Then two members of our group, after protesting unsuccessfully to Father Letellier and to me, went to the White Fathers' Superior, Father Py, whom we shall meet again. The same week, the *quartier réservé* was declared out of bounds for ESSANA.

There was more than one evil in the Casbah. Soon some of us met with drug traffickers. It was a complicated story. I will only say that, when I went to the police, they were politely deaf. Some top people were partners in the business. This time Father Letellier told me to stop inquiring. I did, but I had a particularly warm relationship with a pious old woman who was a kind of doorkeeper to a Marabout, a mausoleum where many pilgrims visited the relics of a holy Moslem man. It was a clean place from which we could contemplate all the cerulean, azure or cobalt hues of the bay and breathe the sea breeze. After a long day up and down the meandering streets, listening to the long tales of misery in stifling rooms or hurrying through the *quartier réservé*, I was glad to have a chat with my old friend there. One day she showed me that she had rashes on her leg. She also observed that the visitors to the shrine were leaving money, but none was left to her who had no sheets. Anyway, with the war restrictions, how could she buy sheets and stop scratching her poor legs on a palm mat? It seemed risky to steal the sheets of our students' home, so I went to plead with the White Fathers. One of them confessed to having three pairs of sheets. I insisted that he would be the worst possible Christian and a shameless capitalist if he did not give me at least one pair for the old, suffering woman. I went off triumphantly with them, promising him eternal life but leaving him no time to think more of it or unstitch the laundry label with his name on it.

Two weeks later an angry telephone call brought me to the White Fathers' house. I found there a very unhappy priest. He had had a visit from several policemen, who proved very suspicious and even impolite. They wanted to know why so much heroin was found in a sheet belonging to this Catholic minister, especially considering that the Marabout keeper said that he had delivered the whole thing for her to hide and had not said what it was. I never saw my old friend after that. She was telling her beads in prison, and one more illusion had left me.

Soon the misery, the squalor, the depths of suffering, violence and vice began to weigh heavily on part of our team and to take some of our strength and youthful optimism away. Once or twice a week, I was among a few helpers in the clinic of the Sisters of Saint Vincent de Paul at the foot of the Casbah hill. I will not describe the desperate cases that came to these courageous sisters with large hearts and little resources. I particularly remember some cancer patients in great pain and total destitution. Cocaine and heroin drugs were cheap but not purified, and there were experiments with various mixtures. For two years many addicts developed a dreadful disease. Their legs and feet were swollen as if they had elephantiasis and deeply infected. Before bandaging the wounds, we had to empty them with a spoon. The sight and smell made me sick, but the sisters were at their work for hours. For the patients, the pain and itching were unbearable, but it did not deter their companions from taking more drugs. I was wondering what human effort could achieve in such lives, such a world? And the war was going on. We had more than our share of bombings. Wave after wave of deep suffering was breaking on our narrow shore of time and space.

One day, when I was rushing down street stairs in the Casbah, I came upon an unlikely party: three Frenchmen in elegant suits having a discussion in a vivacious but friendly manner with two tall Arabs in striped, rather blanket-like garments at the door of one of the rare decent houses of the area. One of the young Frenchmen was not unknown to me. Lucien Paye had an important ministerial office in Morocco in spite of his youth, and I had met him through my father. He greeted me, and we exchanged some jokes on finding ourselves in a place so inappropriate for both his work and mine (supposedly studying philosophy). When I explained briefly about our social service, he became very interested and suddenly bade goodbye to his interlocutors and told me in the easy tone of those used to having their way, "I am curious about this place and your ideas. I will accompany you." I answered that he would not be welcome visiting Moslem women in the absence of their husbands. There, even in crowded situations, a man would not go across a courtyard or a patio where women worked without signaling carefully his presence and lowering his eyes. He would not even speak to women relatives. Mr. Paye laughed and asked me many questions.

When he left me, I could not guess that I would soon receive a strange appointment through the information he had gathered in our conversation. He himself was one day to be the first European ambassador to China; and, after the Red Guards revolution, he became the highest civil servant in France (*Président de la Cour des Comptes*). Once I received two letters from him in a week, which was very unusual. In the first one, he said he was very busy with a project for the reform of the whole organization of television and radio networks in France; and, in the second one, that he had just been told he had an inoperable cancer. He died soon after, all his plans unfulfilled but with the highest hopes in his heart.

Chapter XIV

Typhus

Instead of running ahead in time, I should go back to the time of leaving my parents at the end of 1940, just to say that by then we were very united. Knowing that they were waiting so much to hear from me, I wrote many letters home, to Casablanca, but they never had enough of them. We prudently avoided political comments, as both my father and I were involved in underground activities, and his file in the new French government (Vichy) was in enemy hands. When I returned home for my first holidays, we were awakened by a stone thrown at our shutters. We went to the door. There was nobody there, but a note written in block characters had been left on the floor: "Prepare for arrest." We spent the rest of the night burning compromising papers in a drum. Father refused to go into hiding, because he did not want his friends to be at risk. In the early morning the police were there, and he was taken to prison. Mother could not get any explanation from the plainclothed men who "invited" him to their car and forbade us to follow. Our great fear was that he would be sent to France and executed.

Days of anguish followed for mother in tears, for me in prayer, and for both of us in letter-writing. My father's friends, alerted, made a concerted response. Some of them were still in positions of authority, and he was released. But he was told that he would be in compulsory exile at Oujda, in eastern Morocco, allowed only to teach in a small children's class, with no right to move, publish, invite people and so on. Father asked mother to remain at Casablanca. To follow him was not only to share his dangers but to lose the kind of specialized work she liked to do in transmissions and to live in very uncomfortable conditions, far from her accustomed environment and friends. She said that she would not desert him and added with a valiant smile, "We are lucky to be sent to Oujda. With our daughter in Algiers, we are halfway to her." Oujda is in the same region of extreme tropical climate as the first place in which we had settled in Morocco (Taourirt). We were given a very small house near a school. I was quite proud of my parents. They stood together in dignity, more happy to suffer for their convictions than to join the innumerable converts to the Vichy regime. Father refused the compromises offered to him and each time was in danger of meeting a worse fate.

I returned to my student life. At first I lived with my friends in a kind of hostel and asked Anne to share a room with me. She was a soothing, regulating element in my life, and maybe I introduced some diversity into hers. Her example of sound, traditional Christian living was beginning to bear fruit in my life. It is only through her that I came to know something of the preconciliar Church. I had no love for popular devotions, but somehow it was helpful to go to Benedictions and rosaries on special days or months with so many Christians, as well as to fast and give up concerts and theater or sweetmeats during Lent. We had very few food delicacies anyway, as we were under "restrictions" and experienced war shortages, though not on the scale of European populations. For lack of fuel, our "home" was not heated, and in winter we often studied in bed to save calories.

We were on the fifth floor and our room faced that of Claudine's sister across a paved yard. Between the two French windows there was a long beam made of concrete and about twenty centimeters wide. I did not know what this aerial beam was used for, but it was a perpetual challenge to me. One day I walked across to the window facing ours. It went very well up to the midpoint of the distance separating the two wings. I was walking quickly and with assurance. Twenty centimeters is more than enough for a foot. However, then my friend opened her window and screamed. Other windows opened, and all those fears around me were like winds sweeping me off-balance. I felt dizzy and reached my destination only with great difficulty. Sometime after this experience, I wrote what was called a "successful paper" on the social elements of fear; and I tried the beam again as well as the cornice in front of the building. But before I could make real progress in the interesting art of the equilibrist, I had to save my strength for more useful if not less dangerous activities.

Typhus broke out in the whole of North Africa and the Middle East. It was, or so we thought at the time, the last of those great epidemics that have killed millions of people at each fresh eruption since medieval times. It did not have the same scope as the "Spanish influenza" during the First World War, but it was the same kind of devouring plague, decimating whole households in a few days, striking young and old, rich and poor, and in many places leaving no family without dead. In some, no mourner was left to bury the victims. Typhus is spread by lice, which are very common in North Africa. No vaccination existed then. In Casablanca, one of our comrades died after helping to prepare some crude vaccine with dried lice. He had been very careful in handling the insects but remembered too late that it was also dangerous to breathe their dust. People were so afraid that almost nobody wanted to be near a poor man in buses or queues (there were lots of queues for food, clothing, soap and so on), and nobody accepted willingly to be inoculated after a good number of human guinea pigs died from the experimental vaccine. Then the authorities established a sanitary cordon around the Casbah, where people were dying by the thousands.

Father Py summoned me, and he said that this was the end of ESSANA unless we wanted to be vaccinated. No one was admitted in the Casbah without passing through this ordeal. He warned me of the consequences of both vaccination and disobedience to the new law. Briefed on the prospects, six members of the team volunteered for the inoculation, which was also imposed on the medical staff. Two days later each of us had an enormous shoulder, high fever and other unpleasant symptoms of typhus, but we recovered more quickly than the other patients and were glad to resume visiting our now-imprisoned friends. The days of fever left me weak, however; and it is said that lice swarm on weakened persons.

At first I did not recognize the infestation because it was mostly in my hair. Needing more freedom at night, I had stopped living in the students' hostel. My landlady for a time was Mrs. Scotto, a stern Protestant, who disapproved of my associations, especially since she had recognized a Communist leader among my visitors. She did not give me much in the way of facilities for washing, so I went regularly to a hairdresser. One day he made me pay an excessive price, and, when I asked for an explanation, he answered: "It is because of the lotion" with such a disapproving air that I went to Anne for examination. She was distressed at what she saw and began killing the insects. After counting more than a hundred she told me that I needed a prolonged and drastic treatment. So I turned to Lélou, who had good facilities. Her father was puzzled. "Isn't your friend a little strange? She visits you almost every day now, but she spends most of her time washing! " Lélou did not give the reason for this oddity.

I was not to be lice-free for long: daily trips in the Casbah did not help. There the situation was tragic, and we could do but little. Father Letellier was thinking more and more of a new religious congregation. Another one was being born in Algiers; and I met the foundress of the Little Sisters of Jesus, Sister Madeleine. Typhus vaccine improved slowly, but many still refused it, and the death toll continued to be high. How could one comfort those who suddenly lost their children, parents or spouses? Moslem faith helped, but when one of my fellow students from Morocco, the only child of atheist parents, died, I wondered what words could alleviate their grief. I sent Anne with a message of Christian hope, and the bereaved woman, who until then had been very scornful of our "superstitions", unexpectedly embraced her. She had been one of those who forbade me access to their home after my supposed conversion.

When I arrived at Oujda for the holidays, another girl my age, our neighbor, a very good-looking, healthy young woman, was going happily to a volleyball match in another town. She came back sick and was gone the day after. It looked as if we were going from distress to distress. Still, I was called to witness more suffering.

Chapter XV

France in Bonds

The organization of Catholic Students in France (JEC) was preparing a very important summer camp, in spite of all the opposition and difficulties that the leaders had to overcome in order to ensure a minimum of independence and of necessary means: travel, food, authorization. Each university had to send one or two students. I was elected to represent Algiers. My parents thought that I was invited for academic purposes only, and I did not have the courage to tell them the whole truth. They were anxious enough, as it was not easy to go to France, even to the regions of the country partly free from the German occupation. The war had been very hard on French people. In the towns many were starving. My own uncle lost forty pounds in weight, and, when one photo was smuggled to us, we did not recognize him. Food could be obtained only with ration tickets distributed by the government according to age, sex, and work, and which were insufficient for each category. French meat, milk, coal and iron were going to Germany, as well as the treasures of her art museums.

Our camp was in the Alps, and the peasants there brought us meat and creamy milk. Some of my companions cried because they could not share this bounty with their deprived families.

The very afternoon we reached the mountainous site, in my ignorance of electric trains, I put a foot on each rail. It was a tremendous experience. I felt completely glued to the metal by the strange force. It shook every fiber of my body and especially my heart. I owe my life to the prompt and deft intervention of a student who detached me from the rails with a piece of wood. The chaplain ran to help and told me, "You don't look too strong. Someone must be praying for you. Two days ago a big cow died after having done just what you did when you jumped on these electrified rails." My heart trembled in me the whole night as if it had a life of its own. I missed Mass and the first meeting, but the Jesuits who had organized the camp were celebrating the feast of their founder and had told the students: "No work today: eat and talk." For around fifty youngsters who had spent the whole year starving and silent (as far as politics were concerned), this was a gift!

In the evening I felt strong enough to walk through the bright green meadows. From the snows, half a day's walk from us, hundreds of icy brooks were springing, dancing, jumping, and were supposed to be our uninviting washing pools. While the students were exploring some torrent rocks, I looked at the deserted camp and its dozens of wooden, thatched chalets on short piles. A door was ajar. I pushed it and entered an improvised chapel, which was in fact an unused, carefully cleaned up cattle shed. Jesus is used to cribs. There he was, lodged in a small tabernacle surrounded by fresh mountain flowers. On the uneven planks a primitive altar stood. A priest in a long coat was praying in the shadow of a big beam. I had not received the sacrament of Penance all the time I had been at home and traveling. I asked for it. No threatening box there, and the priest was friendly. He was also curious in a noninquisitive, encouraging way. I told him that I did not know what to do with my life. He said, "You can do many things for God, but he wants only one. It is this that makes a choice difficult. Will you die for him?" I answered, "Yes." We all have this tendency to reach for the offered chalice without knowing what it means. But somehow there was light in the priest's question, perhaps all the light I was to need. I told him then, "I work for people who live in much misery. How can we dare to speak of joy there?" My Jesuit prophet answered, "Take this image of Saint Francis of Assisi and read the beautiful saying at the bottom: 'Joy springs from purity of heart and constant prayer.' A pure heart is a humble heart, and constant prayer is a miracle of love." He said many other things, but I kept only that: the picture of my Father-to-be in my room and the words as a beacon for all the years to come. I knelt down in the sunset and received the Eucharist.

Busy days followed. The young Frenchmen and -women in this camp were being prepared for intellectual resistance. Cardinal Gerlier of Lyons had prepared a clever program, which escaped official censure because it was not understood. The subject of reflection was "The Christian idea of body", but this was the basis for discussion on the evil and stupidity of racism and of all the Nazi philosophy. It was risky but very important at a time when so many European children were exposed to Fascist propaganda. And there was a Jew among us. He was a Frenchman said to have Spanish origins, with a very ordinary Spanish name, Gonzalez. But I had come across in Morocco this kind of Jew who had fled the Inquisition and settled north or south of Spain. Two centuries later in France and in more peaceful times, some of these people became Christians and were practically indistinguishable from their European neighbors. We were perhaps imprudent in discussing his case openly. A few months later our Gonzalez and his mother were killed for no other crime than having some Jewish blood.

Two of the students, both called Jane, were preparing to join a religious congregation. One of them impressed me very much. It was the first time I had seen how beautiful the light of Christ is shining in a young woman in love with him. "You have put a seal on my face that I might never give myself to another love." The sign was there, the sign that I was to see on so many Poor Clares. It was radiant on Mother Elizabeth (Algiers) on the day of her Solemn Profession and gave even more grace to the brown features of a young Malawian girl, now abbess of Lilongwe, when I met with her for the first time, on the feast of the Transfiguration of Christ. Yes, God's love is transfiguring; and I was dimly conscious of this mystery in Jane's smile.

After the camp I went to Lyons to gather information on the Resistance. I also visited slums to learn from the social service there. In one family a half-witted boy was kept hidden, for his parents knew that the German policy of killing "useless" people in hospitals was already secretly applied in some French towns. I also visited Ars . . . , but can we say everything?

The Apostolic Sisters of Mary Immaculate, a religious group in lay clothing, then rare, who worked in the slums, had two guests whose holiness warmed me. They were Oblates of Mary Immaculate, too. One was a sick bishop who had spent long years in an extremely harsh climate. His face was ravaged with deep scars from the cold of the North Pole, but his smile was like the sun on icy cracks. The other one made the most inspiring reflections on the Holy Trinity that I have ever heard and interrupted his mystical speech to inquire if I had remedies and handkerchiefs for the heavy cold that burdened my journey.

These contrasting concerns started me thinking on the originality of Christian holiness.

Down to Marseilles, the train was very hot and very crowded. I listened to a military man who had crossed the boundary of the occupied zone of France (which included Paris and Brittany, from which news was very scarce). He spoke of Germans shooting people for sport, tortured resistants, dying children and also of heroism and solidarity. So we reached Marseilles, the enormous starving city on the Mediterranean shore. Near the "Company of Navigation" a woman stopped me. "Are you going? Have you some food cards left? Please, please! My boy has T.B. and can be saved only with more food." She had a thin, anxious face. I gave her all my cards, and she kissed me for the pound of meat and the extra bottle of milk with a few loaves of black bread that she could buy with them. For me it was hardly a loss. The day after, I was to sail from France, and I had three lumps of sugar in my pocket. I had also secured a room for the night at a kind of hostel run by religious. My food book being empty, I avoided the dining room but slept well enough in a clean room.

I had checked to make sure my boat was due to leave at 10:00 A.M. This left plenty of time for an early Mass at the famous Basilica of Notre-Dame de la Garde, whose golden statue watches over the port and the sea from the summit of her hill. After Mass I greeted our Lady, breakfasted on my bit of sugar and ran down to my boat. I was there at 9:30, but the boat was not at the quay. To my anxious inquiry, a company clerk answered: "We told you to leave your address. But when we telephoned there at six, seven and eight, nobody knew where to find you. We always change the announced time of departure to lessen the danger of being followed by enemy submarines and torpedoed." Our interchange ran:

"Do you have another boat for Algeria? "

"The next one is ten days from now."

"And the other companies? "

"You will be obliged to pay the full fare again."

I did not have the money. I pleaded, "But how can I stay here without food cards? "

The man hesitated. "Well, that is a problem. The only thing we could do for you, though it is not safe and we take no responsibility, is to let you go on a troop transport that leaves six days from now. But it is illegal, and you will not have a cabin."

I accepted gratefully and returned to the sisters, who told me that I might keep the room but that food was not available. After two days of complete fasting, I found something to buy with the few coins I still possessed: a dozen cactus-figs, not real figs but the watery excrescences that grow on some thick thorny leaves, and an ersatz cheese like a small bar of soap and completely devoid of fat. In fact, it was like a piece of plaster in a paper. I ate two little figs a day. At first I spent much time in the church of the Fathers of the Blessed Sacrament. Priests there were always in adoration in front of a huge monstrance surrounded with a profusion of lights and flowers. But soon I was obliged to spare my strength, and I developed boils. Once more it was in an awkward place, this time on my upper eyelid. I was completely disfigured. The sisters sent me to a clinic where the doctor said I needed vitamins and sulfonamides. He could not provide any. Back at the convent I was glad to receive some hot water to bathe my forehead and eyes. Even this was a luxury, as people had no fuel for cooking, and I was fed on the smell of beans and potatoes when I passed near the kitchen.

On the sixth day, I finished my cactus-figs and went to the boat. One of my eyes was completely shut and the other catching the infection. I found myself on a large deck, surrounded by hundreds of noisy soldiers; I thought that, after all, it was providential to be so unattractive, as I was alone in this youthful masculine company. I felt very weak, and, as a tolerated but unauthorized passenger, I was not supposed to get any meal during the two-day journey. I did pray for "our daily bread", but it did not seem to be a successful petition those days. I tried to find at least a place to sit and suddenly felt a hand under my elbow steering me firmly between the moving soldiers and their packs. A tall boy with a blue haversack on his shoulder had taken charge of me. He did not say, "Good afternoon" or "Can I help?" He only murmured in my ear: "I have ship biscuits." Wonderful secret! Leaving France, how could he have these compact biscuits made of real wheat, salt and margarine? He did not tell me, but we shared them happily. It was time I had a meal. And all the more because when night came we had a mini-tempest. The soldiers went to their shelter in the hold, but the few deck passengers remained exposed to the rain and soon to the foam and even the waves that broke over the topsides. After midnight the small bar of the ship was shut, and my companion went to plead with the barmen. He returned to me triumphant. "They say that you may sleep on the table." It was an imperfect bed and an imperfect sleep, but you can be quite happy with only a dry board, a sea biscuit and a new friend.

The boat was going to Oran, where Anne-Marie Baron had a comfortable home in a residential area along the sea, some kilometers from the town. I had wired my date of arrival and was dreaming of the cushions that would welcome me in her gleaming car. What I saw on landing was Anne-Marie with her blond hair on her nose, riding a bicycle and pushing another one toward me. "I thought you would enjoy a bike trip more than a drive in a car." I did not enjoy it, and I almost collapsed in the arms of her mother when I reached their home. The good lady was quicker than her daughter in perceiving my needs, and for a week I was fed, spoiled and rested as never in my life. For the first time, too, I was like a member of this marvelous human and divine reality—a true Christian family. It was not a question of just saying grace before meals and a rosary in the evening but of an affection that had its source deeper than human ties and that, far from making those ties less important and relevant, strengthened and transfigured them.

I was in almost good condition again when I took the train for Oujda. My eyes, however, were still swollen and red, and my mother bathed them a hundred times. She delighted in the exercise, and I restrained my ungrateful exasperation. Being pampered for long has always had a negative effect on my character. My father asked quizzically if I had profited much from my academic meetings and research. He volunteered: "When you want to hide something from us, mind your envelopes. I received a long letter that you intended for Claudine. I am sure that she has read what you wrote to me, and I rather resent it." He let me go to Mass on Sundays without comment, and sometimes during the week I could run to the church and receive our Lord from the priest, who was usually busy with boys in the courtyard. Then I was happy again.

After a few peaceful days, my father fell ill and we called the doctor. He examined him carefully, said a few reassuring words and left his room. Then he called mother and me. He said, "He has caught it." We looked at him in consternation. In those days, "it" meant typhus. The doctor added, "The hospital is over-brimming with this kind of patient. I shall treat him here with your help. Don't panic. But your daughter does not look strong; send her away." I vigorously protested that I had been vaccinated and survived it. He then changed completely. "You will nurse him. But don't let your mother approach. It is not only because of the possible contamination but because these cases are difficult to handle. The patients lose their senses with the very high fever and develop an extraordinary nervous strength. Yesterday one of them threw his wife through the window. It may be better to tie him if he becomes confused or violent." To tie him! I had seen the ugly marks on the legs and arms of my dead friends, and I cried out, "Oh, no! I will manage." "At least", said the doctor, "have a man in the house at night." So we called a neighbor.

The first night my father roamed the house in a state of great agitation. I called our guardian, and I found that "the man" had fled through the window without our patient's help. There was no cure for typhus. The doctor's strategy was to strengthen all the organs attacked by the illness through different kinds of medicines. Some had to be administered several times a day, and I went to my often delirious father twenty-six times in twenty-four hours with pills or potions. It took some perseverance to get him to swallow the prescribed drugs. Sometimes he was saying strange things that appear to me now like Zen *koans*. "For three hours I have been in a queue, but I was the only one there", for instance, or, "In total opposition, unity is perfected." Maybe typhus is good for philosophers. One day he woke up clear in mind and cool in body. What a feast! He was saved. And before we told him his own story, he announced: "After all, this epidemic is taking such proportions, I think it is better to be vaccinated."

My last memory of Oujda is of an invasion of tiny black ants. There were billions of them. Everywhere water can penetrate they could enter. In spite of frantic efforts, every-thing in the house was filled or covered with them. We were ankle deep in the black tide. They overflowed our cups, pans, drawers. They made thick bedspreads when we swept the tables, and they darkened our curtains when we were busy shaking our books. After two exhausting days for us, they left as suddenly as they had come, the whole sea of them. Half an hour after that, we heard a great din of pails and shovels in our neighbor's house.

At the end of September, I returned to the Casbah, the University, the Catholic Association and the Communist Party. There was more to come than I expected.

Chapter XVI

Bombing Raids

November 8 was Anne's birthday. I spent the night in her room so that we might go to Mass together. In the early morning we heard cannons, guns and clamor everywhere. As soon as Anne awoke, I jumped out of my bed in joyful triumph: "The Americans are here! It is surely the Americans!" The good old maid who managed the home screamed excitedly up and down the stairs that we should keep very calm. Some of the students had a guides' camp up on a hill. There bullets whistled around and even through the tents. At last the commotion aroused a girl who had a solid reputation as a good sleeper. She opened one eye and asked, "Is it rain?" Near the post office, our professor of philosophy was busy placing men and machine guns against the "enemy". My Communist comrades began celebrating. The authorities were in high confusion, as was part of the French population after years of Pétainist propaganda. But the great majority of both French and Moslems received the Allies with enthusiasm.

In Morocco, two thousand died in the useless fight, and the Americans won no friends by sending the lowest caliber men from their prisons for the landing. Their activities were in no sense military when they occupied Casablanca, and the Arabs were scornful of these "gangsters".

In Algiers, the United States troops and, some weeks later, the British distributed food to the population. Chocolate still has the taste of freedom for us. Like most of the girls at the University, I soon had American friends. One of them had a beloved fiancée in the States, and I introduced him to different aspects of Algiers and Algerian life. He was the kind of G.I. you see in the pictures, blue-eyed with blond hair, very patriotic, optimistic and candid. I admired his casual relationship with his superiors when off duty, his total absence of self-consciousness at church (I was still far from that), but I was surprised at his lack of interest in the world around him and at his cultural vacuity. In this he was not perhaps typical of his college-level compatriots. I had very little time for dating but introduced him to a group of young people who had interesting meetings. At first he did not enjoy them. Sometimes we spent an evening in discothèques, sometimes in very lively discussions. When the debates were on scientific subjects, I was interested but contributed little. When it was art, it was easier for me. Once we discussed painting as a subliminal process. I left Rembrandt and like magicians to others and sang the praises of "the factory" of Picasso. I loved the golden harmony of the early work of that "monster genius" more than his later sensualist research, and I easily won the tribute I wanted for it. This time my American companion seemed to come to life intellectually and even borrowed art books from the secretary.

I was also interested in chinaware and discovered a very precious vase of seventeenth-century Dutch art in the luxurious villa of a student, a villa that was briefly the dwelling of General Eisenhower some weeks later. Her father, wanting to please me, invited me to dinner and put the delicate pottery with three carnations in it at my right elbow. It was irreplaceable, worth a fortune, and I felt sure that I would push the fragile wonder to the floor the first moment I stopped concentrating on the movements of my arm. My friend said that I never looked more wise and holy, all absorbed in lofty thoughts, than at this dinner.

Time for these leisurely activities was narrowing, however, partly because of the bombardments and their consequences. They might have looked slight in comparison with the London blitz and the destruction of Cologne or of my native town, Brest, which was completely ruined; but for more than two years the Luftwaffe sent bombers over Algiers almost every day and sometimes several times a day. The sirens' scream became a very familiar sound, warning the population of an immediate attack. All life would come to a sudden halt, and crowds would disappear underground. Waves of bombers came one after another, and the dreaded metal eggs began to drop. Explosions were deafening, fires blazed, buildings crumbled, hundreds of people died and thousands were wounded. I was a member of a Red Cross team. When a bomb fell, the center of information telephoned to those of us who were closest to the place of impact. This was often during the night, which was illuminated by the Air Defense (ARP) rockets and the conflagrations. I was not afraid, even when the bombs continued to fall and stones hit my helmet, but I was not a good helper. The sight of torn bodies, crushed children, amputated adults, made me feel weak, even though rarely to the point of fainting. It is then that I learned that the Name of Jesus is prayer and sometimes the only possible prayer. But I still felt that my strength was lost through the victims' wounds. And what can you say to a woman who has just seen her husband, mother and three children killed in a moment? I witnessed such tragedies. Many of the German bombs were *bombes soufflantes*. They destroyed directly the buildings on

which they fell, and the power of the blast made all the
neighboring houses tumble down. You died if you were in
any of them; but if you were in a strong shelter, you usually
survived unless the place was hit directly. So many shelters
were dug or strengthened (most Mediterranean people have
an underground wine cellar). Near the Casbah a big underground tunnel was prepared, but one night a bomb fell close
by and there was a panic. More than two hundred people
were trampled to death, though none would have been
killed by the bomb itself.

I moved to an apartment on the fifth floor of a large
building near the Government General at the center of the
town. A lady there lent me a room when her elder son was
mobilized. Each time we went down to the shelter, obeying
the strident calls of the sirens, she took with her a bag of
jewels, money and securities that she carried on her heart.
And she entrusted me, as if it were a secondary concern,
with her six- or seven-year-old daughter. I often had to
take the child in my arms as we were rushing down the
stairs, and in the shelter I prepared her for private first
Communion.

On Sundays I was often asked with another member of
ESSANA to help a small community of White Sisters who
run an ophthalmological clinic in the suburb of Cervantes.
They also had an Arab team of guides who were difficult to
educate. We did not like the superior of the sisters; she was
very strict and did not admit us to Mass when our hair was
not covered. On a rainy day in November 1942, the siren
rang and the sisters began to descend into the shelter, but
the superior stopped them. "It is time for the rosary. We shall
say it in the chapel, according to the Rule." One sister had
to go to the clinic, and we know these circumstances
through her. All the other sisters were killed a few minutes

later when a small bomb fell directly on the chapel. No one would have perished in the shelter.

Sometimes only the front part of the buildings fell, and, passing in the streets, we could see the stories open like a box of which one side had been carefully removed, with all the furniture still inside the sliced rooms. The house where I lived with the little girl and her mother was half-destroyed in this manner.

I asked the Franciscan Missionaries of Mary, who had a big orphanage on top of the hill of Our Lady of Africa, to lend me a room. They owned a small house half on the slope, half on pillars, with a large view of the splendid Bay of Algiers, where three students could be lodged. The orphanage was on the other side of the massive basilica, and we could not hear the children. There was also a fortress not far away, near the Poor Clares' monastery, and the ARP was operating from there. When there was a raid, our little house was so shaken that my desk and bed traveled from one wall to the other. As soon as the bombing began, we were supposed to take shelter in the sacristy of the basilica, which was very solidly built. One night, having risen twice already, we decided to sleep there. An old visiting White Father came for an early Mass and, finding three girls in pajamas in the sacristy, ran away so fast that we had no time to offer an explanation. We were largely compensated for the fragility of our home by the magnificent sunrises and sunsets on the sea. They made me join the monastic Lauds and Vespers before I knew of canonical Hours.

It was a very sad day in early spring, on April 17, 1943, when a wave of bombers came over the orphanage. The sisters had only one strong shelter, just big enough for all the children to be in some security. They led them there with two religious to keep them safe and happy. The other sisters,

fifteen of them, had to be satisfied with the slender protection of their dining room. The bomb fell. None of the
children was harmed. All the sisters were killed. For some
days a hand or an arm could be found more than a kilometer away. I must admit that I avoided the scene of this
massacre. Many mourned the Franciscan Sisters who had
offered their lives to love and protect the small Arab orphans
who were Christ for them.

As the bombardment increased and the political situation
remained uncertain, with Roosevelt ignoring De Gaulle and
Girault unable to win popularity, the University shut its
doors for a time. All the students from Morocco went home,
but I did not. I did not want to leave all the work in the
Casbah to Anne-Marie and the few Algerian students. I also
preferred to be with Lélou, who was in trouble, and I
needed to be clearer about my call before seeing my parents
again. Mother was very anxious, but soon I had another reason for not leaving Algiers.

De Gaulle, having finally overcome the opposition of
both his friends and his enemies, came to Algiers, where he
gathered a *Gouvernement Provisoire de la République*. I will not
review what is well-known history. He was given the Lycée
Fromentin to establish his headquarters and ministries. One
day I received a very official letter with seals and big head-
lines. It was a summons to Lycée Fromentin. There I found
Mr. Paye, the young, bright man whom I had once met in
the Casbah. He was smiling, assured and a little protective.
He told me that he was *Chef de Cabinet*, something like the
Minister of Education, René Capitant, a notorious *résistant*,
who was also in charge of the social services. Capitant had
appointed me as head of this department for the Region of
Algiers under the former principal (or was she a teacher?)
of the college of Oran, who was supposed to look after the

same services for the whole of North Africa. It looked so absurd that I thought he was making fun of me. How could I, at twenty-one and without any training or competence, provide social services for three million people? He laughed away my objections. I asked if all the departments of his government were staffed in the same way, and he answered: "We try to make some enlightened choices, taking into account our actual limitations; and we believe in a kind of natural selection, some social Darwinism, for the months to come. Besides, the higher you go, the less competence is required. What about a minister who is moved suddenly from Agriculture to Defense or from Industry to Health? You have good ideas on social service. Here is your chance to apply them. You are very lucky; you begin at the top!" I was not convinced. Then he said: "See Capitant himself; he is the boss here." So I was introduced to the Minister. The interview was brief. As soon as I tried to express my astonishment and misgivings, he said, "This is now the French government, and we are at war. You are now mobilized and required to serve in this ministry. Mr. Paye will give you all the necessary information." Mr. Paye did not.

I was given a typewriter and a telephone in a corner of a classroom that had been requisitioned for our ministry. The lady from Oran was greatly annoyed, because she expected me to know what to do, since she herself did not. And she found me too young. She was also fiercely anticlerical; but I was well acquainted with this kind of prejudice, and at the end we got along rather well.

We spent much of our time those first weeks just trying to get information about what existed as social services in North Africa, without any possibility of going to those we were replacing, because they were in prison or in disgrace. Information had to be collected in a piecemeal way, which took much time. Neither did I want to be used in the witch-hunt that soon began. I remembered that one day police had come to our student home (and did not find me) because I refused to have a group of young people sing the Pétainist song, "Maréchal, nous voilà." I was not going to have some naïve teacher or good sister arrested now because she sang the anthem!

There were some glamorous sides to the job: rubbing shoulders in the corridors with important people, sometimes even De Gaulle, whose tall silhouette was at the head of a very long table where sometimes all the Fromentin officials were gathered. De Gaulle, Giraud and the other generals also worshipped together, when they were in Algiers, in a small chapel reserved for them and the Fromentin people. Both music and sermons were beautiful—sometimes. The sharing of information, of ideas about the new future Republic, was interesting. Lélou worked in the Department of Information, where her good command of English was useful, and we were beginning to know more about the Nazi crimes and the state of affairs in Europe. I had no faith in what I was doing. Though apparently very busy, these times were for me empty months; and I did not want my life to be an empty life. I wanted God to fill it, to use it, or to take it, as he chose.

Chapter XVII

The Monastery

I am almost at the end of the only part of my autobiography that I intend writing under my abbess' orders. I had a threshold to pass at this point. In fact I had to lose my life, and what is there to say after that? Everything will be new after the frontier. This frontier, this turning point, was at the Monastery of Saint Clare in Algiers, and so I have to introduce it.

Monastic life, too, has its heraldry, and each monastery keeps track of its history and preserves the archives of its origins. It was Saint Clare herself who sent some of her daughters to found the Monastery of Béziers in the south of France. Reformed by Saint Colette, Béziers in turn founded Orthez, which sent a group of sisters to Azille to revive there a fourteenth-century house of Saint Clare. During the First World War and in tragic circumstances, a young abbess was elected at Azille. Mother Clare of the Sacred Heart had exceptional qualities of mind and heart matched by a strong will that knew how to yield to the Spirit of God. Soon the monastery was overflowing with young women eager to offer their lives to Christ and with him. These did not die in their early twenties as did Saint Thérèse of Lisieux and many contemplative nuns of her generation, because Mother Clare inaugurated a better balance of prayer, work and austerity.

She herself had been very close to an early death for lack of competent care and proper medicines when an excess of hard work, fasting and cold left her with Pott's disease. All her life she carried the consequence of this bone tuberculosis, which ate into her vertebrae. While it impeded her movements, it gave her also a supplement of spiritual vigor. I cannot keep from telling something of the foundation of Algiers. It has much to do with my own vocation.

Mother Clare had been born in a very Franciscan family. Her parents were members of the Third Order, and both her brother and her uncle were Franciscans. Father Pierre Baptiste Gimet, her uncle, was to be Provincial of France, England and Canada. When I visited some of our English monasteries, I found testimonies in their archives of his kindness to our sisters there. He was not only a relative but also the spiritual father of Mother Clare, who inherited his devotion to the Name of Jesus, heralded long ago by Saint Bernardine of Siena. I read a book written by Father Pierre Baptiste himself on *The Powers and Glories of the Name of Jesus*. The front page shows the Bernardine monogram: an angel holding a shield on which are engraved the first three Greek letters of the Name of Jesus, I.H.S., sometimes translated: *Jesus Hominum Salvator*, with a small cross on the Eta, which is written like our capital H. Mother Clare founded three monasteries. It was just after the death "in the odor of sanctity" of Father Pierre Baptiste that the foundation of Algiers was decided on and entrusted to his intercession.

The Archbishop of Algiers had promised spiritual and material help as well as adequate housing. However, when Mother Clare and her six companions arrived in the Mediterranean city in June 1932, they were dismayed to see that their "monastery", which was not even large enough for their small group, was situated in a noisy environment, without a garden and, worst of all, without water! She asked to move and obtained from the Archbishop only a blessing and an order to remain on the hill of Our Lady of Africa. She was severely handicapped by her disease, but the superior of the Jesuits and of the Franciscan Missionaries of Mary proposed to help her in her search. She recommended the recitation of the Litanies of Jesus' Name to her daughters in their mini-chapel and rode in the Jesuits' car. The search was unsuccessful until Mother Clare sighted a white Moorish-style villa in a large garden, on a slope covered with olive and orange trees descending toward the blue bay of Algiers. The place was secluded but not isolated. The villa itself was very beautiful, could be enlarged and had extensive premises. But it was not for sale. However, its owners emerged just when the abbess was wistfully contemplating the house; and as she showed her interest, she was politely invited in. These owners were rich Jews, and before them the house had always been in Moslem hands since its erection more than three centuries earlier. There was a columned and vaulted dining room, which could make an artistic chapel. Another smaller room was also vaulted and decorated. It had been a smoking room for generations of Arab masters to enjoy their coffee and tobacco. On entering there, through a patio graced by a multicolored fountain, Mother Clare was stunned by the sight before her. On a central pillar and the two adjacent parts of the wall, the decoration consisted of three large colored ceramics deeply inlaid into the thick structure: an angel holding a shield engraved with the monogram of Jesus' Name, exactly as printed in her uncle's book. At the same time she heard his voice saying: "It is here that Jesus wants you." The voice was so clear that she looked up, but only her two companions and the two Jews were in the room. To buy the house was a very difficult enterprise, but she succeeded. Since then, the smoking room has become a cherished oratory with its shining ceramics in the wall. The superior of the Jesuits was astounded, too. Some scholars of his Order visited the place. They said that the house had certainly been built by Christian slaves, captives of the Moslems, and probably Franciscan disciples of Saint Bernardine. Their masters never guessed the meaning of these "decorations", but Christ Jesus through them had left his mark for their sisters to discover more than three centuries later.

The ESSANA group went to the monastery for days of retreat from time to time. I heard the story from Mother Clare herself: "It is here that Jesus wants you." I listened to these words as addressed to me. They entered my heart. But this time I said No. I was afraid and unwilling, and more so each time I went to the monastery. It had been completed in a very simple way, but the chapel and the surroundings were still very beautiful. However, I heard that it was considered a fault to look at the sea and that, on the other side of the grille and black veil, the nuns never saw even the priest at Mass or the Host in his hands. I noticed the very low intellectual level of the meditations proposed to them (we could hear the readings from the extern chapel) and knew that the sisters were not allowed even to read the Bible. The life was harsh with daily vigils at midnight, fasting and a lack of modern facilities. All this, of course, has been corrected in our times and even before the Council, though the traditional elements of fervent contemplative life have not disappeared. I was not afraid of poverty and penance, but I did fear the kind of obedience that I could foresee would be imposed on me within this rigid framework. I was proud and filled with many desires and interests. Life was full of promise for me with my friends of Fromentin. Still, I believed deeply in the power of prayer and of the Cross and in the value of a life totally consecrated to a search for God. I breathed an atmosphere of holiness in this house of God and in my conversations with Mother Clare. For months I felt divided and uncertain. When a student listening to the sentimental hymns of the sisters (although most of the time they prayed the beautiful Office of the Church) said, "You cannot spend all your life shut up with a bunch of women of this kind and nothing to do", I was frightened, though I knew that "the women of this kind" were superior to me in all ways that counted.

When I began to go more often to the monastery, my closest friends were less surprised than were more casual acquaintances. One of them had this remarkable reflection: "All right, go ahead. One day we shall be there, too, and you will be our abbess." I forgot the prophecy, but she did not and made me look around me after my first election. Many of my friends had indeed followed Christ into this monastery. One of them, who was later to become Mother Elizabeth, had many questions about the monastery when she knew of my interest. She was delicate in health but strong in her desire to belong to God. Sister Emmanuel, now in Malawi, needed much courage to leave her unwilling and stricken family. Sister Raphael left riches, cherished ties and books (she, too, was a philosophy student). Sister Suzanne, her pencils and brushes . . . for a time. Later on came Sister Germaine, my faithful companion since then, and Sister Henriette, whose Franciscan vocation is blooming and bearing fruit on African soil. Did the Lord not give me back even my little Anne, now Sister Agnes? Yet we were not allowed to speak to one another for many years, and I would not break this rule or any other.

In 1944, my friends were not yet sure of their way, and I had to go alone. It was not my choice, but I knew that God wanted me there. To continue saying No to this call would have been to say No to him, and I could not deny him. After my first spontaneous reaction and a time of hesitation, I yielded to his will and began to long for the silence in which I would be able to worship the Father in spirit and in truth and to be united with the crucified Lord.

Father Eberhard told me to go to a French Carmel with Claudine, as the end of the war was in sight. Claudine did enter there the following year, but I loved Saint Francis for his total truthfulness, and I had heard in that monastery on the hill, "It is here that Jesus wants you." Father Letellier was deeply frustrated. All his plans for the foundation of a new congregation were at stake. He visited Mother Clare and told her, "Don't receive this girl. You don't know her! She will never obey anyone, especially a woman. Just now she may be in the streets with her fist in the air, singing the International." The abbess calmly exhorted her visitor to be more ready to believe in God's grace.

This grace I needed above all for my parents. I wrote to them about my decision. Some time later my father made the visit of some union leaders in Algiers an excuse to come. He was nervous and anguished. No dialogue was possible. I had seen how difficult it is to find comforting words for atheists who lose their only child; but my disappearance into a convent, especially a monastery, was more cruel and incomprehensible than a death for my father, and he told me so. He added that mother might not survive this shock. I was deeply torn. My prayer was dry and difficult, too.

Just when my work at Fromentin was becoming more interesting, I could not concentrate on it. We had many services to organize for people coming from Tunisia and other refugees, for abandoned women, victims of bombardments, and so on. With the little money available, I do not know what the fate of so many distressed people would have been without the silent, persevering, disinterested work of all the religious communities. I admired them, but God had not marked my place among them. I turned more and more to our Lady. When I climbed up the hill to visit the monastery, I often stopped for a long prayer in the basilica of Our Lady of Africa, the black Virgin in a Queen's clothing. It was not rare to find Moslems there, especially woman, all covered with a large white sheet wrapped around them and over their heads. They were telling their troubles to the compassionate Mother of Sidi Aissa (Jesus), and she listened to them.

My favorite Scripture text became Philippians, chapter 2, which proclaims the obedience of Christ unto death; its redemptive value was the core of my faith. I had only the weekends for the Casbah, and then I considered how helpless I would still feel, trying, even for my whole life, to lighten this misery. If only I could be a real friend of Christ, my prayer would touch God, and he, as he alone can, would touch those in need of healing of soul or body. One day at dusk I entered the Moorish chapel of the monastery. Several extern sisters were saying the endlessly repeated Our Father of their Office, and the phrase "Your will be done" recurred like a call to complete acceptance. I was twenty-two that week and told the Lord I wanted to give him my youth. My father had said that, if I entered a convent, not only would he never have any contact with me, but he would intensify his struggle against the Church. Was this also the Father's will? Then I think that I received a promise: faith would come to my parents and even the sacraments, a complete faith as a pure gift from God, the fruit of Christ's death, and not the result of my words or even of my example. I did not make any bargain with God. I was going to him because I loved him; it was unconditional. And although his promise was wordless, as usual in my life, I knew the silent voice of my Shepherd. After that, I felt sure that the very fact that would make my family revolt even more against the Church would lead them and, I hoped, other people, to Christ and to her. I decided to go and see my parents for the last time.

I had first to obtain my demobilization. Lucien Paye was stunned. "You cannot do such a thing! De Gaulle will be in Paris before the end of the year. You have an unbelievable opportunity if you remain with us." When he saw that I was not to be tempted, he remained silent a moment and added, "This will kill your father." I am certain that without God's strength I would not have endured the pain these words gave me, and it long continued to tear at my heart. The papers were signed by the Minister.

On the second of July, while the Church was celebrating the Visitation of our Lady and the Allies were fighting in Brittany, I reached home. My mother had filled my room with fragrant, coral-colored roses. This small attention hurt me much. How could I respond to it when I made them suffer so intensely? Father looked sick. When I tried to speak, I was overcome with tears. There was no way to make them understand or accept. Mother said, "It is for you that I live." They were watching me, but I had to escape. Two days later I left home, leaving a letter on the table. I hid at Claudine's house to avoid pursuit and from Rabat took the train back to Algiers. It was extremely hot, and I was so exhausted on arriving that I could hardly walk to the monastery. I brought nothing with me. It was decided that I would enter the cloister in the evening of the following day: July sixth. I made three resolutions:

—To search for the Face of God not only in prayer but in having no other intention in my work, words or sufferings.

—To obey completely and always, whatever my thoughts or feelings might be, in conformity to Christ obedient unto death.

—Never to complain or to justify myself but to keep Jesus' silence.

I do not know how all this came to me. I have never regretted making the first two promises, though I had many doubts later on about my faithfulness to the first one. The second one probably saved my vocation. Claudine, who entered Carmel and became mistress of novices, finally left religious life. I had the same views and inclinations, but I submitted to all because I believed more in the power of the Paschal mystery than in anything else. Vatican II gave us much of what we wanted, but it was too late for Claudine. My third resolution was very imprudent. Once it led me close to physical death and several times to uncalled-for sufferings. It could have ended in spiritual disaster. It was all right for perfect people, but what I needed was resolutions for beginners. Among those, openness and simplicity are certainly most useful.

God knew, however, that I was just naïve; and suffering taught me little by little the ways of wisdom. I could perhaps have consulted Father Py. He was the only priest who encouraged me, saying, "If you search for God, go in peace to this monastery. It is truly a house of God." But he was then in Italy as a military chaplain in the army of General Juin. He did not know that I would enter the "house of God" in summer. I was very touched when in August I received a card from him. It had been posted at Assisi with the stamp of

July 7 and read: "Assisi is freed at last. Yesterday I said Mass for you at the tomb of Saint Francis." It was the day of my entry.

I was given a pair of long stockings, as my skirt was judged too short, and a pair of gloves, before being dressed in the black sheath of postulants. I looked at the big knobbed door and thought, "I will never cross this threshold again." The Lord may have smiled. Fifteen years later I was to fly to Black Africa, my beloved country, cross many frontiers even in Europe and the equator more than twenty times. Now America invites me through the friendly voice of Mother Francis of Roswell. And yet I have never chosen to travel, even once, as my fifteen years of enclosed life had taught me that, for those who are called to it, a cloister is "the Tent of Meeting" with the Living God. Facing the enclosure door that sixth of July, though, I was sure that I was at the end of my journey on terrestrial roads. A priest said something very pious to "bless my entry". Kneeling in cotton stockings, listening to these still foreign expressions and looking at the veiled forms beyond the threshold, I was conscious of an almost infinite distance between what I was and what I was supposed to be. But the grain of wheat had to be buried. I went to the other side, and an enormous key turned grindingly in the lock.

In my narrow cell when evening came, I felt so tired, bruised and confused that I could not pray. I knelt down in front of a wooden cross: "You wanted me here, and here I am." Then I knew that I had been accepted and that all would be well.

Chapter XVIII

For God Nothing Is Impossible

I have spoken so much of myself that I want to end by turning back to those we have met in these pages.

I have already said that God called some of my friends to the same Franciscan contemplative life. They are still there, hidden springs of living water in the Church of Africa: in Algiers, Malawi and Zambia. Claudine, after leaving Carmel, took up a teaching career. She is successful and unsatisfied. Lélou in Paris has a wonderful family that is also my family. After I "defected" to the cloister, Anne-Marie abandoned the project of a new congregation, but she consecrated herself to Christ privately and continued to work for the Moslems of North Africa and the Middle East in government agencies. She adopted two Arab orphans. Then she felt that they needed a father and tried to find a husband who would respect her vows. God had surely prepared the right (and rare) young man for that. They married, renewed their vows of chastity the same day, and the family stood together for many years.

Father Py became Provincial of the White Fathers in North Africa. He was to encourage me much to undertake the foundation of Lilongwe, saying (I hope prophetically): "This monastery will be a seedbed of contemplative life in Africa." He sometimes asked for his death to be on the pattern of Christ's death, and he was killed by the Arabs whom he loved and had come to help. Father Letellier left the Society of the White Fathers for a time and went to teach in a Moroccan university, but he eventually came back to his brothers.

My grandparents and Tante Jeanne found their way to God in a providential manner while I was still a young religious. Two of them were helped by Sister Therese, a fervent daughter of Saint A. M. Javouhey. She wrote to me that she had been inspired by the Lord to replace me in visiting them in their illnesses. Grandfather Le Goulard was evacuated from Brest when the British destroyed the town to prevent the Germans from using its naval dockyard and port. It was winter, and he died on the way, in a small village. "Little Marie" never left his side, except to call a priest when she saw him very sick. He was still conscious and received the sacraments happily. His sons would never have allowed him to see a Catholic pastor if he had remained at Brest.

My parents had no one to help them, as they had never tolerated a Christian influence around them. My departure left them very bitter and unhappy. They not only refused to have any correspondence with me but for years after threatened to break off relations with any of our relatives or friends if they wrote or even spoke to me. It happened that one of my former teachers who had been away for three years came back to Morocco. She asked my father, "How is your daughter?" He answered the puzzled woman, "You must be mistaken, Madam. I have no daughter."

I was already in solemn vows when Mother Clare saw in the daily news that my parents had narrowly escaped death in a serious road accident in Spain. Father had four ribs smashed into his lungs and mother suffered painful wounds and a leg broken in seven places. They survived their injuries but were obliged to remain several weeks in a small town hospital where the ambulance had left them, in the care of sisters who sent us news of them. They were soon short of foreign exchange, which was difficult to obtain at this time. Mother Clare sent *pesetas* immediately. As my parents had to return them, they were obliged to thank for the service, and thus we came in contact again. They could not remain hostile after reading our letters, and they even visited me in the parlor of the monastery, where they were received with great tact by my abbess and sisters. When I went to Malawi, they began writing to the first African sisters there: our present Mother Josefa, Mother Clare, Sister Mulumba and those who soon joined them, as to their "grandchildren" and to send them parcels. However, they never made a positive allusion to Christianity. I respected their beliefs as they had come to respect mine, and only in prayer did I touch the subject.

They retired to France, choosing the sunny town of Nice but spending most of the summers in Brittany, where they rented a small furnished house in the resort town of La Trinité sur Mer. There Father enjoyed fishing for shrimps and mother eating them; she also occupied herself with knitting artistic cardigans. When a missionary working in Malawi, Father Saffroy of the White Fathers, visited them on my behalf, he told me, "I was well received, but your father has lost nothing of his combative spirit where religion is concerned."

Three months later, in April 1973, father had a slight heart attack. When he recovered, mother wrote: "Lucien is not reasonable. We are only in May, and he wants to drive to Brittany. When I told him that it was too early to be at the wheel for seven hundred kilometers, he said, 'I don't want to die here.' This shocked me. He is not in danger, but he should rest more." They did drive to Brittany. That year I was federal abbess of the Poor Clares of Africa and was obliged to travel extensively, which is very unusual for a Poor Clare. I was almost always alone because it saved money; but this time Mother Josefa was with me. It was a difficult journey. We had air and road adventures and were even reduced to ask professional smugglers to take us to Lubumbashi. At Mbuji-Mayi I received good news from father, but when we arrived back in Zambia I found a message from Bishop Kalilombe: my mother had telephoned to announce the death of my father. I had always been certain that Christ wanted to give himself to him before his death, that he would receive the Eucharist that was so fully the Bread of Life. Did father resist too strongly?

Soon two letters told me more. One of them was from mother and the other from the chaplain of the hospital where my father had been treated in the nearby town of Vannes. In translation it read:

"M. Le Goulard was admitted at the beginning of June, suffering from an infarctus. He was for some time in intensive care. When he was out of danger, I visited him as I usually do with all the patients. The doctor had told your mother that she could be fully reassured and that she needed rest, so she had gone back to her house. Your father spoke of Morocco in a very interesting way. Then he told me, 'It is strange: I fought the Church all my life and my daughter is a religious.' I asked:

" 'Why did you fight the Church? Are you baptized?'

" 'Yes.'

" 'Would you not return to God?'

" 'It is what I want.'

"I heard his confession, which was sincere and obviously prepared with care. I told him, 'You will say the Our Father as a penance and as a beginning of a new life. I will help you.' But he smiled and said the whole prayer with great faith, not only without help but in the new ecumenical translation, which was still unfamiliar to me! He wanted the Eucharist, and I gave it to him. Then I said goodbye, adding that he must be tired but that we would meet again the following day. He answered, "No, you will not find me here.'

" 'Don't think that the doctors will release you so soon.'

" 'I am not speaking of the doctors.'

" 'Oh? You think you might be in danger again? There is no reason. See: we have been together more than one hour and you are still well, but it is time you rest. I will come again as I say. Anyway, you are at peace with God now.'

" 'Yes, thank you, Father, I am very much at peace.' He died one hour later. I was struck by this event. God was there, and I am glad to communicate what I have witnessed and noted."

The news of this death was telephoned to my mother at La Trinité. It was, of course, a great shock for her. She ordered the body to be brought to the house, where the Breton landlady cried because mother did not allow her to put a crucifix or even candles in the room where he was laid. Several members of the family came from Brest, where the funeral (of course without prayer) should take place. Then the parish priest sent a most unexpected message: "'The chaplain of the hospital of Vannes has telephoned me: M. Le Goulard received the sacraments at his own request and while fully conscious. He should have a Christian funeral." This was received with unbelief, but a nurse came and confirmed it. "I was there when Communion was brought to him. I was not pleased because the interview had been too long. The priest left the door open at the end. When I checked the patient just after, he was calm and looked well."

Although completely bewildered, mother was firm: "If Lucien has made such a choice, we should let the priests finish what they have begun." In dissent, most of our relatives and friends left. The parish priest suggested a Mass. Mother thought that the church would be empty, but she found it filled with fishermen with whom my father had been used to have a chat and to whom he liked to render small services. So it came about that this intellectual leftist leader was accompanied on his journey to God by the Christian prayer of modest fishermen.

Father had always been an indifferent businessman. He had left his papers in such disorder that, although I had long ago renounced all rights of heritage, mother could not even be paid her own pension without my signature. I tried to delegate authority to English lawyers in Malawi, but they refused to have anything to do with French lawyers. The bishop said that I must go immediately to solve this difficulty and to see mother secure in a home for the aged.

Two weeks later I was in Nice. Mother told me, in tears, how the conversion of my father made people upset and dumbfounded.

"But why did he not tell me that he prayed? And he had a premonition of his death, too. At least no one can say that he was not lucid or that he was afraid. He was in his full mind and had all his moral strength to the end."

"So, what was it?"

"It was God." She did not hesitate.

"Will you follow him?"

"Not now. I cannot forgive your cousin Josée."

That is another story. I did not want to put any pressure on her and left it at that. After midnight I heard a loud noise in her room and opened the door. She was on a ladder, ransacking the top of a cupboard. I exclaimed, "Mama, what are you doing at this hour?" She turned a perplexed face toward me, "I thought that there was a book here with the act of contrition."

I telephoned to the parish priest of the area, Canon Galléan, saying that mother would visit him. He said, "No, I will come and we can even have Mass at your place. I think that you will soon be returning to Africa. I will come today."

So it was that mother received the Lord in her home after having been estranged from him for more than fifty years. The drawing room made an intimate chapel with a floor of pink marble and Moroccan carpets. In a crystal vase there were roses of coral color like those that made me cry the day I left home. The altar was quite simple, but for me it was the most beautiful of all altars: my father's desk. The chalice rested where he had written his anti-Christian pamphlets. This was the place to thank the Lord:

> His love is strong;
> His faithfulness is eternal.
> *Psalm 117*